Give Me More Money!

By Ron and Caryl Krannich

CAREER AND BUSINESS BOOKS
101 Secrets of Highly Effective Speakers
201 Dynamite Job Search Letters
America's Top 100 Jobs for People Without a Four-Year Degree
America's Top Jobs for People Re-Entering the Workforce
America's Top Internet Job Sites
Best Jobs for the 21st Century
Best Resumes and Letters for Ex-Offenders
Blue Collar Resume and Job Hunting Guide
Change Your Job, Change Your Life
The Complete Guide to Public Employment
The Directory of Federal Jobs and Employers
Discover the Best Jobs for You!
Dynamite Tele-Search
The Educator's Guide to Alternative Jobs and Careers
The Ex-Offender's Job Hunting Guide
The Ex-Offender's Quick Job Hunting Guide
Find a Federal Job Fast!
From Air Force Blue to Corporate Gray
From Army Green to Corporate Gray
From Navy Blue to Corporate Gray
Get a Raise in 7 Days
Give Me More Money!
High Impact Resumes and Letters
I Can't Believe They Asked Me That!
I Want to Do Something Else, But I'm Not Sure What It Is
The Job Hunting Guide: Transitioning From College to Career
Job Hunting Tips for People With Hot and Not-So-Hot Backgrounds
Job Interview Tips for People With Not-So-Hot Backgrounds
Jobs and Careers With Nonprofit Organizations
Military-to-Civilian Resumes and Letters
Military Transition to Civilian Success
Nail the Cover Letter!
Nail the Job Interview!
Nail the Resume!
No One Will Hire Me!
Overcoming Barriers to Employment
Re-Careering in Turbulent Times
Savvy Interviewing
The Savvy Networker
The Savvy Resume Writer
Win the Interview, Win the Job
You Should Hire Me!

TRAVEL AND INTERNATIONAL BOOKS
Best Resumes and CVs for International Jobs
The Complete Guide to International Jobs and Careers
The Directory of Websites for International Jobs
International Jobs Directory
Jobs for Travel Lovers
Shopping in Exotic Places
Shopping the Exotic South Pacific
Travel Planning On the Internet
Treasures and Pleasures of Australia
Treasures and Pleasures of Bermuda
Treasures and Pleasures of China
Treasures and Pleasures of Egypt
Treasures and Pleasures of Ethiopia
Treasures and Pleasures of Hong Kong
Treasures and Pleasures of India
Treasures and Pleasures of Indonesia
Treasures and Pleasures of Italy
Treasures and Pleasures of Jordan
Treasures and Pleasures of Kenya and Tanzania
Treasures and Pleasures of Mexico
Treasures and Pleasures of Paris
Treasures and Pleasures of Rio and São Paulo
Treasures and Pleasures of Santa Fe, Taos, and Albuquerque
Treasures and Pleasures of Singapore
Treasures and Pleasures of South America
Treasures and Pleasures of Southern Africa
Treasures and Pleasures of Syria
Treasures and Pleasures of Thailand and Myanmar
Treasures and Pleasures of Turkey
Treasures and Pleasures of Dubai, Abu Dhabi, Oman, and Yemen
Treasures and Pleasures of Vietnam and Cambodia

Give Me More Money!
Smart Salary Negotiation Tips for Getting What You're Really Worth

Ron and Caryl Krannich, Ph.D.s

IMPACT PUBLICATIONS
Manassas Park, VA

Give Me More Money!

Copyright © 2008 by Ron and Caryl Krannich. All rights reserved. Printed in the United States of America. Previous editions published as *Dynamite Salary Negotiations*, Copyright © 1990, 1994, 1998, and 2001. No part of this book may be used or reproduced in any manner whatsoever without written permission of the publisher: IMPACT PUBLICATIONS, 9104 Manassas Drive, Suite N, Manassas Park, VA 20111, Tel. 703-361-7300 or Fax 703-335-9486.

Warning/Liability/Warranty: The authors and publisher have made every attempt to provide the reader with accurate, timely, and useful information. However, given the rapid changes taking place in today's economy and job market, some of our information will inevitably change. The information presented here is for reference purposes only. The authors and publisher make no claims that using this information will guarantee the reader a job or a higher salary. The authors and publisher shall not be liable for any losses or damages incurred in the process of following the advice in this book.

ISBNs: 978-1-57023-277-0 (13-digit), 1-57023-277-6 (10-digit)

Library of Congress: 2008922100

Publisher: For information on Impact Publications, including current and forthcoming publications, authors, press kits, online bookstore, and submission requirements, visit the left navigation bar on the front page of our main company website: www.impactpublications.com.

Publicity/Rights: For information on publicity, author interviews, and subsidiary rights, contact the Media Relations Department: Tel. 703-361-7300, Fax 703-335-9486, or e-mail: query@impactpublications.com.

Sales/Distribution: All bookstore sales are handled through Impact's trade distributor: National Book Network, 15200 NBN Way, Blue Ridge Summit, PA 17214, Tel. 1-800-462-6420. All special sales and distribution inquiries should be directed to the publisher: Sales Department, IMPACT PUBLICATIONS, 9104 Manassas Drive, Suite N, Manassas Park, VA 20111-5211, Tel. 703-361-7300, Fax 703-335-9486, or e-mail: query@impactpublications.com.

Contents

Preface . . . . **ix**

CHAPTER 1
Talk Money to Power **1**
- Know Your Worth   2
- What's Your Salary I.Q.?   2
- What Are You Really Worth?   5
- Math 101 – Calculate Your Compensation   6
- Let's Talk Real Money   8
- Getting Hired Higher   10
- The Problem With Salaries   10
- Your Guide to Salary Smarts   11
- A Different Approach   13
- Acquire Useful Resources   14
- It's All About Giving Value   15

CHAPTER 2
Myths, Mistakes, and Money in Your Future **16**
- Myths and Realities   16
- 30 Deadly Salary Mistakes   29
- Put More Money in Your Future   32

v

CHAPTER 3
Compensation Trends 33
- Benefits as Compensation 33
- Know the Value of Jobs 34
- Benefit and Security Trends 35
- 30 Important Compensation Trends 37
- Flexibility in Your Future 46

CHAPTER 4
Know Your Worth and Calculate It Right 48
- Valuing Individuals Versus Positions 48
- Calculate the "Going Rate" 49
- Determine Salary Comparables 55
- Conduct Your Own Salary Survey 62
- Document Your Performance 65
- Calculate Your Value and Your Salary Range 67
- Be Prepared 69

CHAPTER 5
30 Rules for Success 70
- Learn and Follow the Rules 70
- Orient Yourself to Job Search Success 71
- Value Yourself Appropriately 75
- Document Your Value 75
- Use Supports 76
- Project an Image of Value and Success 76
- Invest the Employer's Time in You 77
- Ask and Answer Questions Intelligently 78
- Take Notes During Negotiations 79
- Be Realistic and Seek Common Ground 79
- Be Thoughtful and Mindful of the Future 81
- Additional Resources for Salary Success 81

CHAPTER 6
Respond Right to Ads and Applications 83
- Handling the Compensation Issue 83
- Salary Issues 84
- Determine the Value of Jobs 85
- Deal With Your Salary History 88
- State Your Salary Requirements 92
- Respond to Stated Salary Ranges 94

Contents   vii

CHAPTER 7
Communicate Your Value in Job Interviews **96**
- Talking Salary at the Interview   96
- Interviewing Principles   97
- Initiating the Salary Question   102
- Answering the Salary Question   105
- Questions You Need to Answer   107
- Questions You Should Ask   110
- Use Positive Form   112
- Analyze Your Listener   114
- Manage Questions With Positive Content   114
- Overcome Objections and Negatives   117
- Take Initiative   119

CHAPTER 8
Negotiate the Best Compensation Package **121**
- Go For It!   121
- Levels of Flexibility   122
- Negotiating Techniques   124
- Handling Objections to Your Request   127
- Receiving Benefits   130
- The Stock Option Game   132
- Renegotiate the Future   134
- Handling Non-Negotiable Environments   135
- Don't Expect Too Much   136

CHAPTER 9
Finalize the Offer With Attitude **139**
- Take Time   139
- Consider the Offer   140
- Get It in Writing   142
- Accept, Close, and Follow Through   143

CHAPTER 10
Salary Increases, Raises, and Promotions **146**
- The Myth of Performance   146
- Get Performance Raises   148
- Taking Salary Initiative   151
- Threats and Alternative Offers   152

CHAPTER 11
Salary Finder **154**
- Salaries and Salary Ranges   154
- Local Variations   156
- Salaries for 795 Selected Occupations   158

CHAPTER 12
Continuing Salary Success **179**

Index **181**

The Authors **185**

Career Resources **187**

Preface

IT'S NO BIG SECRET – employees walk when money talks. If you've not negotiated your salary recently, chances are you may be underpaid in today's highly competitive job market.

Few job-related activities are so important yet so neglected as salary negotiations. While individuals may do well in learning how to find and perform on the job, they often fail to negotiate an appropriate salary figure that accurately reflects their qualifications for the job and their value to employers. Thinking that salaries are largely predetermined, or feeling uncomfortable or shy talking about money to employers, they accept the first salary offered to them. Yet, the salary they accept today will become a powerful determiner of their future salary increases.

Regardless of how much salaries and salary ranges may vary from year to year, the principles for conducting effective salary negotiations remain the same. These are sound job search and career advancement principles for achieving success in the job markets and employment arenas of today and tomorrow. You should keep them in mind your entire working life.

We wrote this book because we saw a need to approach this subject in a more systematic manner than heretofore attempted. Indeed, numerous myths and mistakes prevent job seekers and employees from taking effective salary action that could translate into thousands of dollars in additional income. Taking compensation as our major focus, we outline the key issues and strategies that are central to valuing positions as well as individuals within organizations. We examine the salary logic of both employers and employees in the process of reaching agreement on valuing positions and individual performance. The result is a book that puts **individual performance** rather than clever negotiating tactics at the center of any discussion concerning salary and benefits. As such, the book should be useful to job seekers, employees, and employers alike who share similar values in the workplace.

If you are first entering the job market, changing jobs, or advancing your career within an organization, you need to directly deal with the question of salary early in your job search as well as on the job. Contrary to what you may think, salary is not something to be left solely to the discretion of employers. It's an issue that involves important **communication**. From the very beginning of a job search to when you leave the workforce, you need to continuously communicate your qualifications and performance to employers who have the power to dispense rewards.

Whether we like to admit it or not, money is important to us and those we work with. In addition to making life more convenient, it helps us **keep score** on how we are doing in comparison to others and it **gives value** to what we do. How much we make tells us something about how others value our skills and abilities. At the very least, you should try to get as high a score as possible with your present and future employers.

The chapters that follow are designed to help you improve your salary score and better keep score for many years to come. If you begin by focusing on what **benefits** you can give employers – rather than what benefits employers can offer you – you will take a major step in the right direction for improving your financial future. Best still, you'll know what you're worth and you'll clearly communicate your value to employers!

Ron and Caryl Krannich
krannich@impactpublications.com

Give Me More Money!

1

Talk Money to Power

ARE YOU MAKING WHAT you're really worth? Do you know how to get accurate salary information related to your work? Are you prepared to talk about salary with your boss or a prospective employer? Could you use some useful tips on how to better deal with compensation issues that could translate into thousands of dollars in additional income in the years to come?

This book is all about talking money to power from a position of strength. It's not about deception, clever tactics, or getting more than what you're worth. Above all, it's designed to equip you with the necessary knowledge, skills, and vision to subtly tell employers to do exactly what our title bluntly states – **Give me more money!**

Asking for money from strangers, especially those who have the power to hire you, is often easier said than done. Whether you like it or not, you must do it if you want to get ahead in the career game. In fact, if you don't speak today's language of compensation – from gross salary and incentivized pay schemes to bonuses, stock options, and equity incentives – you're not talking real money to power nor taking good care of your career and your financial future. Instead, you'll be at the receiving end of the compensation chain where nice guys, and quiet types, often finish last.

In the end, how you talk money to power will largely determine your worth in the eyes of your boss as well as other important people in your life. While you may justify your lack of salary prowess by saying money isn't important, money really is important for valuing your worth vis-a-vis others. If nothing else, it helps you "keep score."

Know Your Worth

You may be worth a lot more than you think – or at least more than what's reflected in your paycheck. If you want to make more money in your present or future job, then this book is for you. If you're not sure what you're worth, or how to handle a job offer, then let's look at what you need to do and make sure you're compensated properly. Let's start by checking your salary I.Q.

What's Your Salary I.Q.?

Do you really know what you're worth in today's job market? Just how well prepared are you to negotiate you next salary or even get a raise? Can you clearly communicate your value to employers? Are you both a knowledgeable and savvy negotiator when it comes to questions concerning money and other forms of compensation?

If you answer "no" or "maybe" to any of these questions, you may be "salary dumb" in today's job market. Take the following quiz to find out how "salary savvy" you might be in talking money to power. Respond to each of the following 27 statements by circling the number to the right: 5 = strongly agree (Yes); 4 = agree; 3 = not sure; 2 = disagree; 1 = strongly disagree (No).

Salary knowledge/behavior	Yes				No
1. I know I'm fairly compensated for the work I do	5	4	3	2	1
2. I have clear salary goals that include several compensation elements that are negotiable with most employers.	5	4	3	2	1
3. I feel both confident and comfortable talking about salaries, benefits, raises,					

and promotions with my bosses and
prospective employers.   5 4 3 2 1

4. I know how several compensation elements
   work in most organizations, such as signing
   bonuses, performance bonuses, cafeteria
   plans, reimbursement accounts, dental
   and disability insurance, 401(k) plans,
   SEPs, CODAs, stock options, flex-time,
   tuition reimbursement, and severance pay. 5 4 3 2 1

5. I'm familiar with the different types of
   stock options and equity incentives
   available with employers these days.   5 4 3 2 1

6. When interviewing for a job, or meeting
   with my boss to discuss compensation,
   I have a list of "must ask" questions that
   deal with salary, benefits, raises, and
   promotions – and I ask them.   5 4 3 2 1

7. I know what I'm worth in today's job
   market compared to others with similar
   skills and experience and in comparable
   organizations and locations   5 4 3 2 1

8. I can quickly find out what others are
   making for the same type of work I'm
   doing.   5 4 3 2 1

9. I know how salaries are figured in my
   company.   5 4 3 2 1

10. I know what others make in my company.   5 4 3 2 1

11. I know what percentage of my total
    compensation consists (or will consist)
    of benefits and perks versus gross salary. 5 4 3 2 1

12. I work in an organization that has a
    regular salary review process which
    is tied to a semi-annual or annual
    performance appraisal.   5 4 3 2 1

13. I regularly review and re-value my job to
    see if the scope of my work has expanded
    beyond the original position description
    for which I was hired.   5 4 3 2 1

14. I can negotiate a salary 5-10 percent higher than what the employer is prepared to offer me.   5 4 3 2 1

15. I understand the different types of stock options and equity incentives offered by employers in my field.   5 4 3 2 1

16. I know what my current compensation package is worth when translated into dollar equivalents.   5 4 3 2 1

17. I'm prepared to negotiate more than seven different compensation options.   5 4 3 2 1

18. I have a list of at least five accomplishments and a clear pattern of performance which I can communicate to prospective employers.   5 4 3 2 1

19. I'm prepared to tell at least five different one- to three-minute stories about my proudest professional achievements.   5 4 3 2 1

20. If asked to state my "salary requirements" in a cover letter or on an application, I know what to write.   5 4 3 2 1

21. I know when I should and should not discuss salary during an interview.   5 4 3 2 1

22. I know what to say if the interviewer asks me, *"What are your salary expectations?"*   5 4 3 2 1

23. I know what questions to ask during the interview in order to get information about salaries in the interviewer's company.   5 4 3 2 1

24. I know when it's time to stop talking and start serious negotiations.   5 4 3 2 1

25. I know how to use the "salary range" to create "common ground" and strengthen my negotiation position.   5 4 3 2 1

26. I know how to use silence to strengthen my negotiation position.   5 4 3 2 1

27. If offered a position, I know what to
    say and do next.   5   4   3   2   1

                          TOTAL [   ]

If your total score is 80 or less, you are probably under-compensated as well as unprepared to negotiate your next salary. Moreover, you will most likely repeat this pattern in your next job since you are unprepared to deal with compensation issues and negotiate a final job offer. You definitely need to work on developing "salary savvy" skills. If you score a perfect 135, congratulations; you are probably doing very well in the compensation department. Loan this book to a friend who may need it more than you!

What Are You Really Worth?

What are you worth, and how can you get top dollar in today's job market? This two-part question remains a central concern for many job seekers and employees who really don't know their worth; who believe they may accept a salary beneath their true value; who feel uncomfortable talking about money with people of power; and who believe they may be under-compensated for the work they do. Put simply, they don't deal well with the key issue affecting their financial future – talking money to power.

The salary you accept today will largely determine your salary tomorrow.

You may be under-valuing yourself because you lack adequate knowledge and sufficient initiative to deal with money matters. Indeed, most people are probably under-compensated by 10 to 20 percent. They literally cheat themselves by failing to do two important things concerning their value. They fail to:

- Understand and calculate their true worth.
- Value specific jobs and employers.
- Consider compensation alternatives.
- Properly negotiate the highest possible compensation.

Here's one of the most basic realities of salaries: the salary you accept today will largely determine your salary tomorrow. Therefore, over a 10- to 20-year period you may be underpaid by $100,000 to $200,000, or perhaps more. If you lose a thousand here and a thousand there, after a while it adds up to real money!

We're sure you can think of several things you could do with an extra $100,000 to $200,000. Pay off the mortgage? Get the kids through college without taking out a second mortgage? Invest more for your retirement? Take some wonderful trips? Support your favorite cause or charity? If you can't think of anything, let us know. We can show you where to shop for some really neat stuff as well as identify needy causes and groups you can support that can change your salary expectations, and your life, forever. Better still, they could motivate you to acquire more salary knowledge and take greater salary initiative!

Math 101 – Calculate Your Compensation

Before addressing specific issues involved in negotiating salary, let's look at what you're really getting paid at present as well as what you would like to get paid in the future. Start by calculating your current total compensation package by combining your **salary** figures with **benefits** and **perks** you now receive.

Before you negotiate a salary, repeat this exercise by considering all elements that comprise your desired compensation package; assign a dollar figure to each element. Keep in mind that most elements may be negotiable. Some elements, such as supplemental pay options, may be more negotiable than base salary which for many employers may be relatively rigid in structure. Use the following checklist to inventory your total compensation. Start by asking yourself these four questions:

1. Which compensation elements are most important to me?
2. Which elements does the employer offer?
3. How does each element with this company translate into real dollars for me?
4. Which elements are negotiable with this employer?

Talk Money to Power

	Dollar Equivalent	Very Important			Not Important	

Direct Compensation

- ☐ Base salary $ _____ 5 4 3 2 1
- ☐ Bonuses $ _____ 5 4 3 2 1
- ☐ Cash in lieu of
  certain benefits $ _____ 5 4 3 2 1
- ☐ Commissions $ _____ 5 4 3 2 1
- ☐ Overtime $ _____ 5 4 3 2 1
- ☐ Signing bonus $ _____ 5 4 3 2 1

Benefits

- ☐ Cafeteria plan
  (benefit options) $ _____ 5 4 3 2 1
- ☐ Reimbursement accounts $ _____ 5 4 3 2 1
- ☐ **Insurance:**
  - ☐ Medical $ _____ 5 4 3 2 1
  - ☐ Dental $ _____ 5 4 3 2 1
  - ☐ Life $ _____ 5 4 3 2 1
  - ☐ Disability $ _____ 5 4 3 2 1
- ☐ **Financial/Retirement Plan:**
  - ☐ 401(k) plan $ _____ 5 4 3 2 1
  - ☐ Simplified Employee
    Pension (SEP) $ _____ 5 4 3 2 1
  - ☐ Cash or deferred
    arrangement (CODA) $ _____ 5 4 3 2 1
  - ☐ Pension/annuity $ _____ 5 4 3 2 1
  - ☐ Profit sharing $ _____ 5 4 3 2 1
  - ☐ Stock options $ _____ 5 4 3 2 1
  - ☐ Stock purchase plan $ _____ 5 4 3 2 1
  - ☐ Stock bonus $ _____ 5 4 3 2 1
- ☐ **Days off:**
  - ☐ Holidays $ _____ 5 4 3 2 1
  - ☐ Vacation days $ _____ 5 4 3 2 1
  - ☐ Sick leave days $ _____ 5 4 3 2 1
  - ☐ Personal leave days $ _____ 5 4 3 2 1
  - ☐ Maternity/paternity
    leave $ _____ 5 4 3 2 1
  - ☐ Family leave $ _____ 5 4 3 2 1

Perks

- ☐ Flex-time $ _____ 5 4 3 2 1
- ☐ Child care $ _____ 5 4 3 2 1

❑ Tuition reimbursement	$ _____	5	4	3	2	1
❑ Training opportunities	$ _____	5	4	3	2	1
❑ Free parking	$ _____	5	4	3	2	1
❑ Car or car allowance	$ _____	5	4	3	2	1
❑ Expense accounts	$ _____	5	4	3	2	1
❑ Laptop computer	$ _____	5	4	3	2	1
❑ Cell phone	$ _____	5	4	3	2	1
❑ Mobile communicator	$ _____	5	4	3	2	1
❑ Internet account	$ _____	5	4	3	2	1
❑ Paid travel for spouse	$ _____	5	4	3	2	1
❑ Company credit card	$ _____	5	4	3	2	1
❑ Frequent flier miles	$ _____	5	4	3	2	1
❑ Free meals	$ _____	5	4	3	2	1
❑ Free or discounted memberships/services	$ _____	5	4	3	2	1
❑ Discounts on company products	$ _____	5	4	3	2	1
❑ Sabbaticals	$ _____	5	4	3	2	1
❑ Incentive trips	$ _____	5	4	3	2	1
❑ Moving and relocation expenses	$ _____	5	4	3	2	1
❑ Office with a window	$ _____	5	4	3	2	1

TOTAL ☐

Let's Talk Real Money

In American culture we are taught not to ask other people about how much they make. That would be rude, impolite, and insensitive. What you make is your own business – and your employer's business. It's a secret everyone tries to keep, but one everyone would like to uncover about others. It's the subject of gossip, rumors, leaks, organizational politics, envy, and backbiting. Surprisingly, we do a very good job of keeping our salaries and incomes secret from our colleagues, co-workers, friends, neighbors, and even family members. Only you, your employer, your spouse, the IRS, and perhaps your mortgage company, mother, or ex-spouse really know how much you make. In the meantime, we probably speculate about other people's incomes through such superficial visual cues as the size and quality of their homes, cars, dress, lifestyles, and other worldly possessions. While these cues may be accurate reflections of their incomes, they do not give you the total picture of how much they really earn.

Given all this secrecy and intrigue surrounding compensation, many people understandably suspect they are not making what they really should. Moreover, they feel powerless about affecting their on-the-job income. After all, you accept what's given to you if you want to get or keep your job.

Right?

Wrong.

You can probably do better. You can achieve the power to affect your financial future with your employer by knowing what you should be making and by following a few simple rules for negotiating your salary.

How, then, do you know what you're really worth in a society which doesn't readily share salary information? And if you don't know what your co-workers make, how will you know if you are being fairly compensated?

We know it's not a good idea to directly approach someone and ask them *"What do you make?"* While this question is quite acceptable in many other cultures, especially in Asia and sometimes even in California, it doesn't go down well in most of America. Such a question makes others feel uncomfortable as well as brands you as someone who is rude and nosy. And we know most people try to avoid rude and nosy people who make them feel uncomfortable.

But there are other, less intrusive ways to get at the salary question. Every year, for example, numerous salary surveys are published on "who makes what." While some of these surveys primarily focus on the salaries of Fortune 500 executives who make $500,000 or more each year, other surveys cover a wide range of jobs. Unfortunately, most of these surveys generalize for the nation as a whole rather than identify differences among regions. Architects in New York City and Los Angeles, for example, make a lot more money than architects in Peoria, Illinois or Billings, Montana.

Government employees and public school teachers are probably the most well informed about salaries – they have access to published salary schedules that list all salary increments by grade and step. Some even work in places where their individual salary is public information. And some occasionally find their names and salaries published in the local newspaper when an enterprising reporter decides it would make good copy for a slow news week. These employees know where they and many of their co-workers "fit" on that official and highly publicized salary schedule. No secrecy here – just some jealousy about so-called non-meritorious compensation. Their major concern is with annual salary increments as well as the comparability of their "public service" salaries to private sector salaries. Therefore, the government periodically conducts "comparability" studies to identify how much government salaries lag behind those in the private sector. Public school teachers prefer to compare the salaries they receive in their school district or institution with salaries offered in other school districts or institutions. In so doing, they learn how much they are worth given the "going rates" found elsewhere. The concept of "comparable worth" that generates comparative salary surveys will give them a fairly accurate estimate of how much they should make, give or take a few thousand dollars.

If you are neither a government employee nor a teacher, how do you determine what you are really worth? Where do you go to learn about your value and how do you value your worth? We'll address these questions shortly with some practical guidance and examples.

Getting Hired Higher

But knowing what others make is no guarantee that you will make the same. In fact, you may quickly discover the salary averages are nothing more than the summary of large ranges. For example, an average salary of $50,000 a year for an administrative assistant position may mask the fact that the real range for this position is actually $20,000 to $80,000 a year. Knowing that the average is $50,000 may not help you when you are offered $24,000 a year!

In addition to knowing what others make, we also need to know what you and the job are worth as well as how to best respond to initial salary offers that may be beneath your expectations. The process of **valuing** jobs and your capabilities and communicating this value to employers involves researching jobs, positions, and organizations and developing effective interview and salary negotiation skills. The linking of salary information to these special job search and salary negotiation skills is what this book is all about.

The Problem With Salaries

Most people are under-compensated not because employers exploit them. Rather, they are under-compensated because they fail to adequately deal with the salary question. Indeed, many applicants are skilled at writing resumes and conducting job interviews, but they fidget and fumble when asked about salary. Many just take what is offered, because they believe that is all there is; the job is worth what's being offered; or they feel uncomfortable talking about money. They also believe what employers tell them about salaries – they can only pay what is budgeted for the position and the "going rate."

Most job seekers and employees are **unprepared** to deal with the question of compensation. They lack both information and skills for clearly communicating their value to employers. Indeed, they are unprepared because they:

> *Most people are under-compensated, because they do not adequately deal with the salary question.*

1. Don't know what they or their jobs are worth.
2. Fail to conduct basic salary research.
3. Know little about the employer and the company, including its market value.
4. Don't know how to effectively negotiate salaries – from what to say to when and how to talk about compensation.
5. Believe what employers tell them about salaries.
6. Focus on the wrong issues relevant to compensation.
7. Confuse their needs with the employer's needs.
8. Fail to understand the needs of employers.
9. Say the wrong things at the wrong time.
10. Fail to continuously communicate as well as demonstrate their value on resumes, in job interviews, and on the job.

In other words, they are prone to making numerous **mistakes** about what they should be paid. Repeating these mistakes many times over their worklife, they literally lose thousands of dollars in potential earnings.

Your Guide to Salary Smarts

Most people can improve their ability to address the question of compensation by both learning what they and the job are worth and acquiring some basic salary negotiation skills. By linking comparative salary information to particular jobs and employers, they should be able to negotiate higher salaries. At the same time, they will better demonstrate their value and competence to employers by addressing the salary question within the context of their performance and capabilities.

Rather than relegate salary to the category of something you would rather not talk about, the issue of salary should become the central focus around which both you and the employer assign **value** to the job and your performance. By focusing intelligently on salary and compensation, both you and the employer better define the job and your position within the organization. You will know what you are expected to do and how you will be evaluated.

> *Salary should become the central focus around which both you and the employer assign value to the job and your performance.*

That is the purpose of this book – show you how to value your worth, negotiate the best salary possible, and go on to realize your true worth. Our concern here is not with "winning" any so-called salary game through positive thinking, gamesmanship, manipulation, or clever negotiating skills. Such "winning approaches" may be detrimental to your job since how you negotiate your salary with an employer often sets the tone for your continuing relationship; communicate your cleverness by playing hard ball here and you can expect to play hard ball on the job, with you probably losing in the end. Instead, our concern is with **communication** – how to best communicate your qualifications, value, benefits, and performance to employers in exchange for status, position, money, and extras. That's what our salary negotiation techniques are all about.

Put another way, we want you to locate jobs that are at your best level of capabilities and to communicate your value to employers in the most favorable financial terms possible. If you can do this, you will be able to negotiate the salary you deserve. For in the end, you will do both the employer and yourself – as well as the job and organization – a favor by addressing this salary question head-on with information, professionalism, tact, and demonstrated capabilities.

A Different Approach

Our approach to this subject is different from other examinations of salaries. First, we place the salary question within the larger **context** of the job search, employers, and organizations. An important principle operates here: good salary negotiation skills are based on a firm job search foundation involving knowledge of what you do well and enjoy doing – your strengths, values, goals – in order to be better able to communicate your value to employers. This is much more than just another *"you can negotiate anything"* game. It is first and foremost a **process of communicating value** from start to finish in a job search as well as on the job. For in the end, how well you negotiate your salary may determine how well you get along with the employer and your job.

> *Good salary negotiation skills are based on a firm job search foundation involving knowledge of what you do well and enjoy doing.*

Second, to be most successful in addressing the salary question, you need both information and skills. The **information** comes in two forms:

1. Information about salary issues and negotiations.

2. Information on comparable salary ranges relevant for the jobs you seek.

Therefore, the first 10 chapters of this book address salary issues and the salary negotiation process. Chapter 11 examines key resources for determining salary ranges, including a listing of median annual salaries for 795 jobs. While some readers will find the first 10 chapters most useful, others will be primarily oriented to the information in Chapter 11. However, we believe you need to relate both pieces of information in order to be most effective in addressing the salary question.

The **skills** you need are primarily research and communication skills. They focus on gathering and exchanging information about you, the employer, the job, and the organization both during your job search and on the job. Our emphasis here is on developing skills that you will continuously use throughout your worklife rather than on transitory skills that are only used during a 30-minute salary negotiation period once every three to five years. This is a long-term capability that hopefully you will use again and again in the process of continually communicating your value to employers and then translating that value into even higher salaries.

These "salary success skills" should become for you what salary survey information and the performance appraisal skill are for employers. Better still, your salary skills should be aimed at incorporating the employer's salary information and performance appraisal criteria into the process of determining compensation.

Acquire Useful Resources

Each year millions of job hunters turn to career planning books for assistance. Many begin with a general book and next turn to resume and interview books. Others begin with a resume book and later seek other types of job resources, including letter writing and networking books. Some go directly to computer software programs or visit various Internet sites for producing resumes and preparing for job interviews.

If this book represents your first career planning book, you may want to supplement it with a few other key books. Many of these books are available in your local library and bookstore or they can be ordered directly from Impact Publications (see the extensive Career Resources section at the end of this book – pages 187-195). Most of these resources, along with hundreds of others, are available through Impact's comprehensive online bookstore and resource center:

www.impactpublications.com

Impact's site also includes new titles and job search tips for keeping you in touch with the latest in career resources. You also can request a free copies of their career fliers by sending a self-addressed stamped envelope (#10 business size) to have it mailed to you. Send your request to:

Impact Publications
ATTN: Free Career Fliers
9104-N Manassas Drive
Manassas Park, VA 20111-5411

It's All About Giving Value

You have special value that should be adequately compensated. You can make more than you do at present without having to change jobs, careers, or employers. You do so by learning the secrets of conducting effective salary negotiations. While few employers intentionally exploit their employees, most employers only give what they have to give. And what they have to give is largely determined by the "going rate" for comparative positions and by what you are willing to accept.

As long as you willingly accept the "norm" and say nothing about your special value, you will get what you are informed you are worth – the "norm." If you want your employer to pay you more than what he or she initially offers, then you must clearly communicate your special value to the employer. Only **you** can communicate this special value.

No one wants to reward you for your need or greed. Employers want value, and they are willing to pay for it.

Forget playing games, manipulating others, and being super clever. No one wants to reward you for your need or greed. Getting a higher salary is very simple. Employers want value, and they are willing to pay for it. Your task is to know what you're worth and then make sure you clearly communicate your value to the employer. So give it to them!

2

Myths, Mistakes, and Money in Your Future

FEW PEOPLE ARE PREPARED to effectively deal with salary issues during job interviews. Most make errors that weaken their negotiating position. Even fewer handle money questions well once they are on the job. Part of the problem is how they view themselves, jobs, positions, employers, and issues relating to money. They believe in many myths that prevent them from taking effective salary action. These myths, in turn, lead to many mistakes relating to the money question. And these mistakes tend to under-value one's true value in today's job market. In the long run, these myths may cost you thousands of dollars in lost income.

Myths and Realities

Let's examine some of the major myths and realities relating to compensation. If some of these myths make up your belief system, you may want to re-examine your beliefs so they are more in line with the realities. Better still, you may want to change your salary negotiating behavior to focus on those things that are really important in determining compensation.

MYTH 1: **Since salaries are largely determined by employers, there is little I can do other than accept the salary figure offered me.**

REALITY: Most employers work with **salary ranges** rather than specific figures for positions. Although they may be constrained by rigid pay systems and budgets, they do have some flexibility in determining how much money they will offer for a particular position. The low end of the range will be for individuals who meet the minimum requirements. The upper end of the range will be for attracting individuals with better than average experience. In some organizations the range for a position may be very wide, reflecting a difference of $10,000 to $30,000. For other organizations the range may be only a few hundred or a thousand dollars. The initial offer you receive may be at the bottom of the employer's range. Your goal should be to identify this salary range and put yourself at the top of the range by convincing the employer that you are worth being paid top dollar. How you write your resume, conduct a job interview, and negotiate a compensation package will largely determine where you will fall on the employer's salary range.

MYTH 2: **Everything is negotiable. If I can only learn how to effectively negotiate, I'll be able to use this skill to get a much higher salary than initially offered by an employer.**

REALITY: Some things are negotiable, including many salaries. Other things are non-negotiable, including many salaries. The popular notion that everything is negotiable is simply false. For a salary to be negotiable, you must first have a **willing partner**, one who is sufficiently **motivated** to engage in a haggling game. If the other party doesn't need or wish to negotiate, then you have no one to play this game. And some people simply don't negotiate or negotiate very little all; some are even insulted by the fact that you might even consider negotiating what to them is a "done deal." Indeed, many employers have rigid pay systems that do not allow much flexibility on base pay; they may have more flexibility with benefits. Unfortunately, much of what is written about salary negotiations is most appropriate for large profit-making corporations with 5,000 or more employees and for employees who make over $100,000 a year. Since very few people ever work for such organizations or make that much money, much of the advice is inappropriate for most people (85 percent) who work for small organizations (those with fewer than 100 employees) that have less negotiating flexibility on salaries. In fact, many salaries are non-negotiable. The most negotiable salaries are for high-level positions in large corporations requiring a great deal of experience. Even in these organizations, most entry-level positions come with set salaries that are either non-negotiable or involve little salary flexibility. Therefore, if you are first entering the job market or seeking an entry-level position, don't expect to find many employers willing to negotiate your salary.

The popular notion that everything is negotiable is simply false.

MYTH 3: **Higher salaries tend to go to those who know how to negotiate their salary.**

REALITY: Salaries are normally assigned to specific **positions** – not just given to people who demonstrate good negotiating skills. Except in very small organizations, where the duties, responsibilities, and performance of positions are not well defined – jack-of-all-trades positions – most employers assign specific salaries to specific positions. The amounts assigned are normally the going market rates – similar amounts assigned to similar positions in other organizations. Many small organizations have little flexibility on salaries even in the middle to upper ranks. The same is true for government positions which are assigned ranges on a progressive salary scale. Salaries are pre-set for these positions. The only way to significantly increase your salary in this case is to negotiate the level, grade, or step of the position. You do this by demonstrating that your experience qualifies you to enter at a higher grade level. Your most significant salary increase will come when you **change positions**. Consequently, you are not likely to substantially increase your present salary if you stay in your current position. If you desire a significant salary increase, it's best to concentrate on moving to other positions which have higher salaries assigned to them. Unfortunately, many small employers have a limited number of positions to which you may move. You may experience long-term "job and salary lock" because of your inability to move into higher paying positions. In such cases changing positions may mean you must change employers. Compensation for most sales positions involving commissions is determined by one's job performance rather than by negotiating a salary.

> *Major salary increases usually come when you change positions.*

MYTH 4: **I should primarily concentrate on whether or not I will enjoy the job rather than be concerned about how much I will be paid.**

REALITY: You should have no problem finding numerous jobs you will really enjoy. However, many of these jobs pay poorly. Money is important not only for your lifestyle but also as an indicator of your worth. You will do both yourself and your employer a favor if you demonstrate your value and then require the employer to adequately compensate you for your talent. If you fail to address the salary question forthrightly, you may not be respected by the employer who manages to hire you for much less than you are worth. Individuals who can demonstrate their value to employers by translating it into a respectable salary are more likely to do well on the job, because they emphasize what is most important to employers – job performance. Make sure you get paid for performance rather than the "going rate" or a cost-of-living adjustment.

MYTH 5: **The salary I will be offered will reflect what I am worth.**

REALITY: The salary you will be offered will most likely reflect a number of factors, few of which have anything to do with your skills, abilities, and potential performance. Employers normally try to pay the "going rate" for jobs and positions. Some may even try to pay as little as possible, depending on how individuals respond to their offers. Employers determine the going rates for salaries by surveying salaries offered for comparable jobs in similar organizations. Your task should be to clearly communicate to employers that they should factor in your value when making salary decisions. Hopefully, you will convince them that your value is well above the going rate.

> *Employers normally try to pay the "going rate" for jobs and positions.*

MYTH 6: **I'll have a better chance of getting the job if I don't ask for much money; I don't cost as much as other candidates.**

REALITY: This is the "penny wise, pound foolish" mentality of extreme bargain shoppers who transfer the same mentality into the job market. While some employers might find hiring the cheapest candidate attractive, most do not, since they are shopping for quality employees. And quality is not cheap. Most seasoned employers believe the old adage that "you get what you pay for" when hiring people. Their experience confirms this belief. They may pay little for inexperienced people in entry-level positions, but they do so because they don't know what they are getting until the person establishes a track record of performance. Most employers look for **value**, and they give respect to those who price themselves accordingly. If you are too cheap, employers will not see value in you. You will not receive the initial respect you need to get started on the right foot with the employer. Ironically, within certain limits, the higher your price tag, the more value you communicate to employers.

MYTH 7: **Once I prove myself on the job, I'll be in a better position to negotiate a higher salary.**

REALITY: Unless you somehow become very indispensable to the organization – the employer simply can't function without you – and threaten to quit, the initial salary you get may determine what you receive in the long run, regardless of how well you perform on the job. Once you accept a salary, you may have little or no leverage in future salary negotiations. Beware of self-delusions and ego trips to nowhere. Most people think they are worth a lot more to others than they really are. While many feel they are indispensable to the organization, in the eyes of most employers, everyone can be replaced; and many experienced employees are replaceable at lower salaries. When push comes to shove in salary negotiations, many employees who threaten to quit unless their salary demands are met are politely shown the door!

MYTH 8: My annual salary increase will reflect my job performance. Therefore, it's important that I work hard and do well on the annual performance appraisal.

REALITY: Unless you have a written agreement that states your future salary increases will be based on performance – and you know the exact mechanisms that will be used to measure your performance and how they are linked to pay increases – your annual salary increases are more likely to reflect cost-of-living increments than your work efforts. How hard you work, or how well you do on an annual performance appraisal, may only determine whether you are retained or fired. Once you are hired, don't expect employers to carefully calculate your future salaries based upon any performance criteria. Indeed, few annual performance appraisals are tied to salary considerations. Even the concept of "merit pay" is not widely accepted nor practiced in most organizations. To do so might create more internal political turmoil than it's worth, since many employees would feel others had unfair advantages because of their close relationship with their supervisors. Therefore, the best and safest salary strategy for most employers is to give all employees across-the-board salary increases reflecting a combination of cost-of-living increases, bonuses, and profit sharing. Employers are better off providing other forms of recognition – especially psychological strokes – to those who score high on the annual performance appraisal, such as a letter of appreciation, plaque, or an award for "best employee of the month."

> *Once you accept a salary, you may have little or no leverage in future salary negotiations.*

Myths, Mistakes, and Money in Your Future 23

MYTH 9: **I should never discuss the issue of salary during an interview.**

REALITY: While it is always best to keep the discussion of salary to the very end – after you know more about the job and you've established your value with the employer – this is not always possible. Some employers will probe about your salary expectations early on in order to screen you in or out of their salary range. When this happens, be prepared to discuss salary within the context of **ranges** appropriate for the type of position you are interviewing for. Do not state a specific salary figure you expect, since such a figure should be the very last item you agree upon as part of your job offer. At this stage, let

> *You want to be honest, but you don't have to be stupid.*

the employer know that salary is important to you; that you have done your research on salary comparables; that you expect to receive a salary appropriate for your level of qualifications and experience; and that you want to be compensated on the basis of performance rather than on your past salary history or because of need or greed. What you want to do at this point is get a better idea of what qualifications, experience, and performance are required for this job so you and the employer will have a better idea of what both you and the job are worth. Discuss the salary question at any time, but don't finalize the discussion until you have all the information necessary to determine what will be the best salary for you.

MYTH 10: When I receive a job offer, I'll have a job.

REALITY: You only have a job when you've agreed on a compensation package. In other words, you don't have a job until the employer agrees to give you money in exchange for your talent. You need to get a job offer in writing, which spells out your compensation package.

MYTH 11: If asked to state my "salary requirements" on an application or in a cover letter or resume, I should be honest and tell them what I want.

REALITY: You want to be honest, but you don't have to be stupid at the same time! By stating a salary figure, you may prematurely eliminate yourself from consideration, because your salary expectations are either too high or too low! The best response to this question at this stage is that your salary requirements are either "open" or "negotiable." If pressed for a specific salary figure, try to turn the question around (*"What do you normally pay for someone with my qualifications?"*) and then give a range that should be appropriate for the position. You should have salary range information based upon your research of comparable salaries.

MYTH 12: Job benefits are often more important than the gross salary figure offered.

REALITY: While many employers mix salaries with benefits in their discussion of a compensation package, it's to your advantage to separate salary from benefits and negotiate each, starting with your salary. Indeed, some employers may emphasize their excellent benefits, but many do so in order to make their low salary offer look more appealing. Most jobs come with the same or similar package of benefits. Examine the benefits carefully, but settle on a salary figure first. After reaching a salary agreement, turn your attention to the benefits. Consider benefits as something that are expected to come with the job rather than as a part of the salary consideration. If the benefits offered do not meet your minimum standard of what should come with the job, be sure to cost out the missing benefits and include these figures in your salary calculations.

MYTH 13: **I should concentrate on the gross salary figure rather than on benefits when discussing my compensation package.**

REALITY: Yes and no, depending on the particular employer. According to U.S. Department of Labor studies, 44 percent of total compensation for the average worker comes in forms other than base salary. While Social Security makes up the largest portion of "benefits," numerous other benefits can make a significant difference in one's total compensation package. For example, if an employer offers stock options and you know you are with a growing company, the value of your stock could actually exceed your annual salary. Be sure to value **all** of your benefits and include them in a "total compensation figure." In the case of many small businesses that offer few benefits, you may want to concentrate on the salary figure. However, the trend among most employers in a boom economy is to offer more and more benefits as well as incentivize pay in order to both attract and retain top talent. Many employers may have more flexibility in increasing benefits than in raising base salaries. When considering benefits, follow this checklist:

> *Examine the benefits carefully, but settle on a salary figure first.*

- ❏ Bonuses
- ❏ Commissions
- ❏ Overtime
- ❏ Reimbursement accounts

- ❏ Insurance (medical, dental, life, disability)
- ❏ Simplified Employee Pension (SEP)
- ❏ 401(k) plan
- ❏ Pension/annuity
- ❏ Profit sharing
- ❏ Stock options
- ❏ Vacation days
- ❏ Personal leave
- ❏ Flex-time
- ❏ Child care
- ❏ Discounts
- ❏ Tuition reimbursement
- ❏ Training opportunities
- ❏ Free parking
- ❏ Frequent flier miles

Taken together, many of these benefits can add substantially to the value of one's total compensation package, and especially if they are tax-free or tax-deferred benefits. Indeed, a $60,000 salary with one employer may be worth $75,000 with benefits, whereas another employer's $60,000 salary may be worth over $100,000 with benefits. If you add incentivized pay provisions, total compensation could be considerably more.

MYTH 14: **If I am willing to accept a low starting salary, chances are I can increase my salary substantially within the first year by demonstrating my value to the employer.**

REALITY: The most important salary you will negotiate is your starting salary. Unless you are accepting a lower salary in lieu of promising stock options and equity incentives, whatever you accept at this point is likely to live with you for a long time. Most employers are not interested in renegotiating a salary you have already accepted. While they may allude to the possibility of a substantial raise in the future, chances are they have short-term memories when you later discuss a raise. The only way you can substantially increase your salary on the job is to move into another job that pays more. This means convincing the employer that you should be promoted to another position that pays more. You do this by demonstrating that you will do well in a higher level position.

MYTH 15: The best companies to work for offer stock options and equity incentives to their employees.

REALITY: Over eight million Americans now receive stock options and equity incentives as part of their compensation package. However, many of these individuals accept lower salaries in exchange for such compensation schemes which may or may not eventually translate into real money. Many of these individuals also tend to work for high-risk companies – those that have an uncertain future, especially dot-com companies engaged in e-commerce. Most of these companies will not survive beyond the first two years of venture capital funding. But if you choose the right company that goes public and you exercise your stock options in a timely manner, you could become very wealthy. Indeed, this is the new road to wealth for many people who used to believe the only way to get rich is to own a business! On the other hand, many such companies go out of business or their stock options never amount to much. If stock options and equity incentives are important to you, make sure you thoroughly research the company. What's the probability the company will ever go public? What is the real value of your stock options given the current value of the company? Are you willing to take a lower salary in exchange for stock options with what may be a very risky venture?

MYTH 16: **The longer I work for a company, the more I will be rewarded financially. If I change employers, I'm likely to make less because I'll lose my seniority and benefits.**

REALITY: The longer you work for a company, the higher the probability your salary will fall behind the salaries of more recently hired personnel who enter the organization at a higher salary level. Your best salary is likely to be your starting salary. After that you will most likely receive yearly salary increments figured as a percentage of your base. Therefore, your starting base salary will be a major determiner of future salary increments. The longer you stay with a company, the more likely you will fall behind others who have been hired more recently. The only ways to substantially increase your salary are to be promoted to a higher level position or leave the company and negotiate a new salary with another employer.

MYTH 17: **I should let my supervisor initiate actions relating to raises and promotions.**

REALITY: While it is always preferable to have your supervisor take such actions, you must also seek visibility beyond your immediate supervisor as well as among your co-workers. Let others know – especially your supervisor's boss – that you are a producer. Remember, supervisors do change, and personal conflicts with some can stall your career. A co-worker today could well become your supervisor tomorrow. Therefore, it's best to cultivate positive relationships at all levels within your network.

MYTH 18: **Money will not make you happy; it's best to pursue other values that will make you and those around you happy.**

REALITY: Neither will poverty. Unless you don't know how to spend it, money can bring you and those around you great happiness. This happiness "argument" is a good rationalization for not doing as well financially as one could or should; it's an excuse for low achievement. And you will be especially unhappy when you learn you are being paid less than you're worth or receive less than others in the organization with comparable experience. There's a lot of truth to the saying that *"Those who think money can't bring happiness don't know where to shop!"* You'll be especially happy when you get a salary commensurate with your value. While money may not make you happy, it makes life much more **convenient**. Better yet, it helps you **keep score** on your level of success in the world of work. The higher your salary, the more value you have to the employer and the better your score. Don't undersell yourself because of some beliefs about the role of money in life. It's okay for talented people to make lots of money, constantly score high, and live a convenient and comfortable lifestyle.

> *Those who think money can't bring happiness don't know where to shop!*

30 Deadly Salary Mistakes

If myths were not enough to prevent people from dealing adequately with the salary question, many people also make numerous mistakes concerning salary. The major mistakes include:

1. Avoid facing the salary issue until the question about *"your salary requirements"* is raised by the employer.

2. Fail to deal intelligently with salary questions and issues by not doing research on salary comparables, employers, and compensation options.

3. Don't know how much you're really worth.

4. Specify a single salary figure when asked *"What are your salary requirements?"*

5. Assume your "qualifications" and "performance" will automatically determine your salary level.

6. Think salaries are predetermined by employers.

7. Believe you are indispensable to an employer who will give you substantial raises rather than risk losing you to the competition.

8. Under-value your worth.

9. Over-value your worth – may even think you are irreplaceable to the employer.

10. Think the employer is in the driver's seat when it comes to negotiating salary.

11. Approach salary negotiations from a perspective of need or greed rather than as a process of assigning value to your qualifications and promises of performance.

12. Personalize salary issues by believing a salary is assigned to you rather than to your position. Focus primarily on yourself rather than on the position to which salary is normally assigned.

13. Fail to compile **supports** for a negotiating position.

14. Negotiate salary and benefits over the telephone or through e-mail.

15. Prematurely discuss salary before acquiring information on the job or before communicating your qualifications to employers.

16. Don't know how to close and follow up the salary negotiation interview.

17. Forget to consider benefits, perks, stock options, and equity incentives as part of the compensation package.

18. Put too much emphasis on benefits rather than concentrate on the gross salary figure.

19. Project an image that is not commensurate with the salary being negotiated.

20. Put too high a price tag on yourself without providing supports to justify the salary figure, such as previous salary history or indicators of performance.

21. State a specific salary expectation figure on either your resume or in your cover letter.

22. Too quick to accept employers' first or second offers.

23. Don't know how to use **timing** as part of establishing your value in the eyes of employers.

24. Fail to adequately assess the employer's needs and develop a strategy to meet those needs as well as relate this strategy to your salary requirements.

25. Don't give yourself much room to negotiate.

26. Fail to raise intelligent salary questions about the job and the employer.

27. Don't know how to handle employers' salary questions or say the wrong things.

28. Don't know when to leave a job or company for opportunities elsewhere that will pay better.

29. Try to play "hard to get" when you have little or nothing to leverage.

30. Lie about your past salary history or alternative salary offers.

Put More Money in Your Future

The following pages are designed to dispel these myths as well as help you avoid the many mistakes made by others when dealing with compensation questions. Our overall emphasis is on how you can best communicate your qualifications to employers as you eventually translate your value into an acceptable salary for both you and the employer. If you can do this, you should be well on the road to achieving higher salaries in the years to come. While this money may not bring you happiness, at least it will add greater value to your qualifications as well as help you better keep score on your progress in the job market as you continue to advance your career!

3

Compensation Trends

SALARY IS ONLY ONE, albeit the most important, component of employee compensation. When dealing with the salary question, you need to focus on the larger issue of compensation. What exactly goes into a compensation package and what are some of the most important compensation trends that could affect your salary future? Let's answer these questions before you specify your value.

Benefits as Compensation

While many employers separate salary from benefits, other employers view the two together as a "compensation package." For them, a salary may only comprise 60 percent of what may be an attractive package of employer-sponsored health, life, and disability insurance; paid vacations and leave; education and training opportunities; child care services; generous stock options and profit sharing; and an early retirement plan. For other employers, salary may comprise 90 percent of total compensation. In fact, the U.S. Department of Labor reports that total compensation for most hourly workers is nearly 40 percent more than their hourly pay. For example, if you make $20.00 an hour, your employer pays another $8.00 an hour in benefits which translates into $28.00 an hour in compensation. For many people, compensation packages appear confusing and somewhat mystical.

Know the Value of Jobs

When dealing with the question of salary, be sure you know what the total compensation package looks like as well as how much it is worth in dollar terms. While most benefits come with the job and thus are not negotiable, some may be negotiable, especially in situations where employers offer flexible benefit options. Moreover, the benefits offered by one employer may add up to a substantial financial advantage over the compensation packages of other employers.

During the last three decades the trend has been toward increasing employee benefits at a higher rate than salaries.

Information on the total salary and benefit package is important for comparing compensation among employers and for determining how much a **position** is really worth in comparison to other positions. A $50,000 salary with one employer, for example, may be part of a $62,000 compensation package, whereas this same salary makes up most of a $55,000 compensation package with another employer. For during the last three decades the trend has been toward increasing employee benefits at a higher rate than salaries. In general, base wages remain the most inflexible element in compensation packages. Large and progressive companies have led the way in expanding employee benefits.

However, this 30-year "benefits" trend is undergoing significant changes, which should continue over the coming decade as base wages receive greater attention in employee compensation packages. Indeed, employee benefits appear to be under attack everywhere as employers increasingly cut back on what are now viewed as extravagant and escalating benefit packages. The first and most important benefit being targeted for change is health insurance. This is by far the fastest escalating and most costly personnel expense for employers. More and more employees should be prepared to pay an increasing share of their health insurance premiums themselves in the decade ahead.

Benefit and Security Trends

Much of the history of worker compensation is a 20th century story of how government and employers took greater responsibility in ensuring the income, health, and old age security of workers in the form of benefits financed through payroll taxes, retirement funds, and shared employer-employee benefit programs. Prior to the 1930s, most workers primarily worked for hourly wages. Insurance and retirement plans were largely the responsibilities of workers who, at best, needed to save for their own retirement as well as find private forms of health, disability, and life insurance.

All this began to change in the 1930s with the advent of government-sponsored social security and the increasing role of private insurance companies and pension organizations in providing protection against the income, health, and old age insecurities of the workplace and life in general. Such legislation as the Social Security Act and the Wagner Act of 1935 put in motion new wage and benefit initiatives, financed largely through payroll taxes, that have continued to the present day. Protection against income insecurity was primarily seen as a government and employer responsibility. Employees participated indirectly through shared financing systems. By moving primary financing responsibilities to government and employers, the costs of such programs were cut dramatically as workers participated in group benefit plans.

The initial emphasis on income protection against the twin problems of old age and unemployment expanded to cover a variety of other worker benefits during the post World War II period: paid holidays and vacations, insurance, pensions, wages, hours, working conditions, bonuses, stock options, and savings plans. Indeed, the general trend during the past 40 years has been to increase worker benefits at a much faster rate than wages. Consequently, benefits make up a larger share of compensation packages today than 40 years ago. Most compensation packages also reflect the structure of a pre-1970s society in which a male head of household was the sole wage earner providing for a non-wage earning spouse and children. Insurance plans, for example, providing coverage for all family members continue to be central benefits for many workers.

Much of the credit for developing the benefits side of employee compensation packages must be given to the role of unions and the collective bargaining process. At the height of their membership in 1945, when over 35 percent of the workforce was unionized, and throughout the 1950s, unions pressed for greater benefits along with higher wages. However, union membership began to steadily decline starting in the 1960s to where only about 12.1 percent of today's workforce belongs to unions. As the economy in the early 1980s went through a major recession, with unemployment hitting 11 percent, and with numerous plant closures in declining industries, unions shifted their emphasis toward greater job security for workers threatened with layoffs and permanent displacement. Indeed, salary "give backs" and benefit reductions became new elements in the collective bargaining process as unions reluctantly accepted wage and benefit decreases for assurances of long-term job security.

> Cost containment became a major issue for employers who were paying escalating health insurance premiums.

At the same time, new initiatives centering around retirement programs, such as lump sum payments to encourage early retirement, and flexible benefits, were instituted in many companies, including government. As a health care financing crisis loomed in the future for most health care programs, cost containment became a major issue for employers who were paying escalating health insurance premiums. Consequently, more and more health benefit programs shifted from 100 percent employer financing to shared funding by employer and employee. Some two-tiered benefit programs were also instituted wherein newly hired employees received fewer benefits than those already working in the organization. However, these initiatives have not become widespread and many will most likely disappear in the near future.

While wages during the 1980s did increase, the changes were incremental, largely reflecting cost-of-living increases due to inflation. Benefits began to be restructured in response to the changing nature of the American workforce – the advent of working spouses who received similar and often overlapping benefit packages – and the high cost of health care.

30 Important Compensation Trends

The 1980s was a major watershed period for the evolution of wage and benefit policies. Several structural changes in the economy and population placed into motion new trends for compensation packages in the 1990s and beyond. The major impetus for these changes during the early 1980s were poor economic conditions coupled with an ailing economy in need of major restructuring in the face of a highly competitive international economic environment. Other significant developments impacting on compensation included the changing structure of the American family; declining union power; dying industries; the deregulation of transportation and communication industries; skyrocketing cost of medical care; and a bulging national deficit. While some of these changes would continue into the first part of the 21st century, others would be transformed by a new and booming full-employment economy at the end of the 1990s and beginning of the 2000s, which witnessed the rise of more and more innovative compensation packages to attract scarce talent in a new talent-driven economy.

The most important trends for salary and benefits appear to be in the following 30 directions for the coming decade:

1. **Employers will offer more flexible compensation packages:** Given the evolution of the two-career family, where spouses have similar benefit coverage, more and more employers will offer flexible compensation packages and reimbursement accounts that provide options for their employees. The key concept here is **options**. Compensation packages will be structured so they can be custom-designed around the needs of different types of employees. For example, more and more companies will offer their employees a menu of benefits from which to choose: life, health, and long-term disability insurance as well as cash, personal leave, and child care services. An employee who already receives health insurance coverage on his or her spouse's policy might elect to take a cash option rather than receive duplicate health insurance coverage. Such flexibility will be most prevalent in large companies.

2. **Salary increases will be more closely tied to cost-of-living increases:** Regardless of all the talk about performance appraisals, merit pay, and rewarding individual productivity, few employers will actually institute compensation policies tied to such performance criteria. Cost-of-living increases will continue to be the major determinant of salary increases for current employees in most organizations. Performance will most likely continue to be rewarded with bonuses, promotions, and other forms of employer recognition other than salary increases. The single most important factor determining major salary increases for individuals will be a job promotion within an organization or a job change to another organization. These are the times when salary negotiations play a central role in determining compensation.

> *Performance will most likely continue to be rewarded with bonuses and promotions.*

3. **"Give back" trends will continue in declining industries:** As unions remain focused on guaranteeing long-term job security in declining industries, employees in such industries will continue to accept employer demands for lower salaries and scaled-down benefits in exchange for job security. As economic growth slows and unemployment increases, greater attention will be given to cutting back benefits which have escalated in recent years. Even in booming economic times, troubled start-ups and dot-coms will continue to ask their employees to take pay cuts.

4. **Salary caps will continue to pay an important part in depressing top government salaries:** Regardless of all the self-serving comparable salary studies emphasizing that compensation of government employees lags behind those in the private sector, legislators will continue to put caps on the highest salaries paid in government at the federal, state, and local levels. These caps will further deter "the best and the brightest" from pursuing long-term government careers.

Compensation Trends

5. **The highest salaries and most attractive benefit packages will go to such high-demand occupations as chemical and petroleum engineers:** Salaries generally follow labor market supply and demand trends. Occupations experiencing major labor shortages tend to offer higher salaries. The lowest and least negotiable salaries tend to be for entry-level positions as well as those with an over-supply of job applicants. Individuals first entering the job market with few marketable skills should expect to encounter many "take it or leave it" salary and benefit situations.

> *Employers attempt to be both equitable and secretive in determining salary increases.*

6. **Few employees have bargaining power to substantially increase their base salaries and benefits in most organizations:** Once hired, most individuals have little say in determining their salary increases unless they possess critical, hard-to-replace skills and could readily leave for greener pastures. However, most people are replaceable. Employers attempt to be both **equitable and secretive** in determining salary increases. The equitable strategy results in treating all employees the same on the question of salary – give them cost-of-living increases as a percentage of their base salary. This equitable strategy is also an administratively expedient one that best conforms to the rigid pay systems found in many organizations. It is also politically expedient should employees discover how much other employees in the organizations received in comparison to them.

7. **Compensation packages will increasingly reflect the changing nature of the workforce, society, and economy:** Greater emphasis will be placed on flex time, day-care services, parental leave, unpaid leave, benefit options, and employee contributions to the escalating cost of health insurance, stock options, and equity incentives.

8. **More emphasis will be placed on salary increases as the benefit share of compensation declines:** While the past two decades was a period for expanding benefits, the early 21st century will see more attention focused on salaries and increasing the portability of retirement benefits. Therefore, negotiating salaries will be more important than examining benefit packages which will be largely predetermined and similar for most organizations.

9. **Salary negotiations most often occur for high-level professional and technical positions:** Most blue-collar and lower-level professional and technical positions, many of which are entry-level, involve fixed salaries that are only negotiable within very narrow ranges. High-demand positions, as well as high-level positions that are most important to organizations, will have the greatest salary flexibility. Individuals applying for these positions can expect to negotiate salary and benefits.

10. **Salaries and salary ranges will be most difficult to identify for professional and technical positions:** The salaries for most blue-collar and lower-level professional and technical positions are relatively easy to identify given the public nature of these salaries. State and local government agencies regularly gather salary data on these positions, and many classified ads state the salary ranges for such positions. However, publicized compensation data on higher-level professional and technical positions are not so readily available. Consequently, you must conduct your own research in order to identify the salary ranges for such positions.

11. **Retirement plans will increasingly emphasize portability and early-out options in both the public and private sectors:** The old "golden handcuff" pension systems of limited portability will give way to greater portability so that employees can more readily change jobs and careers. Defined contribution retirement plans, largely replacing the traditional defined benefit plans, will enable employees to more easily transfer accumulated retirement benefits with one employer to

another. Declining industries, including government, will increasingly offer employees early-out retirement options in order to reduce ongoing payroll obligations.

12. **Life, health, and disability insurance payments will increasingly be shared by both employers and employees:** The health care insurance crisis in particular will lead the way for restructuring traditional insurance benefits. More and more insurance programs will require greater financial contributions on the part of employees. If implemented, a costly national health care system will likely result in lower salary increments for employees, because employers will have to contribute more to the cost of health care.

13. **Unions will continue to play a minor role in the structure of compensation packages, although some unions may well transform themselves into new labor forces in nontraditional occupational areas:** The decline of unions, which began in earnest during the 1970s, is likely to continue among its traditional bases – agriculture and manufacturing. Labor-management relations will become more cooperative as labor and management agree to collaborate more on productivity and compensation issues. At the same time, we expect some resurgence in union membership as many unions expand their operations into nontraditional occupational areas, especially services, where they will play an increasing role in structuring compensation packages for their members. In fact, from 2006 to 2007 union membership increased from 12.0 percent to 12.1 percent of the American workforce.

14. **Collective bargaining will increasingly be dominated by employers who largely determine the structure of compensation packages.** As union membership continues to decline and new employee-employer collective bargaining mechanisms evolve, expect employers to play the dominant role in the collective bargaining process.

15. **Except for high-demand occupations, employers will be reluctant to negotiate salaries and benefits in today's highly volatile economy:** Salaries will be largely pre-deter-

mined, within narrow ranges, for most positions. Employers will be unwilling to pay more than the norm unless they experience serious difficulty in recruiting new personnel.

16. **Initial starting salaries will continue to be the major determinant of future salary increases for most employees:** Your starting salary will be your most important salary today and tomorrow. Most employers will continue to figure salary increases as a percentage of an employee's base salary. Therefore, it's imperative that you start at the highest salary possible, because this initial salary will affect future salary increments within the organization. Unless you become indispensable to the organization or receive a major promotion, the next time you will receive a significant salary increase is when you quit your job and get hired by another organization that is willing to pay you a substantially higher salary.

> *Start at the highest salary possible, because this initial salary will affect future salary increments.*

17. **Continuing labor shortages will have a significant impact on the structure of salaries and benefits:** Most of the labor shortages predicted for the coming decade will be concentrated at the lowest level of the labor force – unskilled hourly workers who receive minimum wages. While some wage inflation will take place at this level, due to supply and demand problems, increases in compensation at this level will be insignificant compared to other segments in the labor force. Expect to see increased wage inflation at the higher end of the job market – for those with high-demand technical skills. Top-level executive compensation should continue to escalate, with greater attention focused on stock options and equity incentives.

18. **Child care benefits and parental leave will become more important elements in compensation packages:** Family care benefits, including eldercare, will increasingly play an

important role for two-career couples who are concerned that their jobs and careers not be detrimental to their family situations. The demand for liberal parental leave for both men and women rather than the traditional maternal leave for women will become part of compensation packages along with innovative child care benefits. Unpaid leave will become an important issue for employees with dependent care responsibilities – the birth of a child or illness of a child, spouse, or parent.

19. **Reimbursement accounts will offer employees new options for reducing their taxes as well as increasing the extent of employer-financed benefit coverage:** More and more employees will negotiate reduced salaries for the tax advantages of reimbursement accounts that will pay their share of insurance premiums, health care deductibles, and child care.

20. **Cost containment for medical insurance will continue to be a major issue in the decade ahead and will be reflected in differential compensation packages:** The cost of medical care will continue to outpace increases in the general cost of living. Given the high costs of medical care, health and disability insurance benefits will be the most highly sought after employee benefits. Many employees will be less concerned with their overall salary figure than with the percentage coverage of, and the employer contribution to, the health insurance package. Employers, in turn, will continue to push for restructuring health benefits so they include a larger employee contribution to the cost of premiums. Compensation differentials between employers who provide 100 percent medical coverage with no deductibles and those who only provide partial coverage with some deductibles may be great, depending on the family health needs of individual employees.

21. **More and more employers will offer cafeteria plans:** Cafeteria plans let employees choose between receiving cash, which is taxable, or selected benefits, which are nontaxable. The menu of benefits might include health and accident insurance, medical reimbursements, dependent career assistance

payments, disability insurance, and group term life insurance. There cafeteria plans represent a "win-win" situation for both employers and employers since they reduce tax liabilities for the company (FICA and FUCA) and the employee (gross income). Many employees will elect to receive such benefits; they have greater value than cash because they are provided through nontaxable dollars.

22. **More and more employers will offer their employees long-term investment opportunities for retirement planning:** The growing popularity of Simplified Employee Pensions (SEP) and 401(k) plans will continue as employees take advantage of new opportunities to develop an individual retirement account, annuity, or a cash or deferred arrangement (CODA).

23. **Supplemental pay will continue to play an important role in compensation systems:** Basic salary will remain the most rigid form of compensation. Once a pay system is in place, including upward adjustment policies, few employers have any interest in altering it in response to individual circumstances. Instead, employers have greater flexibility in offering lump-sum payments, nonproduction bonuses, profit sharing plans, reimbursement accounts, and overtime in addition to the base pay rates. These supplemental pay options will continue to expand in the decade ahead in response to the compensation needs of different employees.

24. **More comprehensive and flexible paid leave policies will be offered by employers:** More and more companies will adopt flexible annual leave policies that give employees opportunities to accumulate and defer paid leave for different leave situations – personal, sick, vacation, military, funeral, holiday.

25. **More innovative and attractive compensation packages will be developed as recruitment strategies in a highly competitive labor market:** The coming decade will witness major labor shortages due to a slow-growing labor force with

fewer young people entering the workforce. In efforts to recruit from this dwindling pool of traditional entry-level employees, more and more employers will emphasize attractive compensation packages, complete with bonuses, savings plans, child care, educational benefits, and health coverage.

26. **More and more contingency workers will enter the job market primarily for the purpose of acquiring attractive benefits rather than for receiving significant salaries:** A growing army of temporary workers that are leased or contracted out to clients will continue to expand. Since limited but attractive benefits are offered by firms managing such workers, more people will be attracted to such working arrangements which also give them the advantage of a flexible work life.

27. **Small businesses will compete more favorably with large businesses on compensation packages:** More and more small businesses will contract out their compensation packages to firms specializing in group benefit programs. Operating like large businesses, small businesses using these arrangements will be more competitive on the benefit side of compensation.

28. **The fastest and most rewarding way to increase your salary and benefits in the decade ahead will be to own a successful business:** The coming decade will continue to be an explosive period for new businesses. More and more individuals – many talented and successful people who lost their jobs due to downsizing and early retirement – strike out on their own in starting businesses. The successful ones will realize incomes beyond their fondest dreams. Their compensation will far exceed the limited salary and benefits they received when they worked as "salarymen" on other people's payrolls. Best of all, they have no need to negotiate their compensation since **they** are the boss. While stock options and equity incentives will still be important concerns for salaried employees who dream of getting rich by exercising their options, such a "road to riches' plan will be no substitute to starting your own business.

29. Most salaries and benefits will be inadequate for supporting the traditional family with a single head of household: The number of two-career families will continue to increase in the coming decade. As salary increases lag behind general cost-of-living increases, more and more families will require two or three income sources in order to cope and prosper financially.

30. Executive-level compensation increases will continue to accelerate in the coming decade: Top executives can expect to see 10-30% annual increases in compensation, which will considerably out-pace the salary and benefit increases of all other employees in their organizations. The salary gap will continue to widen between highly paid executives and all other employees.

Flexibility in Your Future

These 30 salary and benefit trends raise several important issues you need to consider when addressing the compensation question with potential employers or with your present employer. No longer is compensation a simple issue of how much salary and how many paid vacation days you will receive. Compensation today deals with complex social issues that reflect the changing structure of American society and the workforce. These issues affect most workers, be it medical insurance, child care, unpaid leave for dependent care, paid leave, education and training reimbursements, portable retirement systems, early retirement, or reimbursement accounts. These benefits can add up to a sizable proportion of one's compensation. Indeed, you may discover that 30 to 40 percent of compensation with some employers comes in the form of benefits.

The key dynamic in compensation packages today is **flexibility**. More options and more choices will continue to be offered in the decade ahead as employers adjust to a restructured society and workforce of the 21st century.

At the same time, don't expect to negotiate many benefits with employers. While some employers will have flexible benefit packages that enable you to select from a menu of choices, most benefits come with the job. What you most need to know is your **options** and how these options add up in terms of total compensation. With this information, you can

Compensation Trends

compare one employer to another and decide whether the $50,000 job offer with Employer X is equivalent to the $50,000 job offer with Employer Y. Indeed, you may discover that Employer X's $50,000 is actually $55,000 whereas Employer Y's $50,000 means $62,000 in total compensation.

These compensation differentials are also important for your future earnings power. For example, when employers ask you for your salary history, you need not state $50,000 since your total compensation package translates into a much higher dollar figure. Instead, talk in terms of the cash equivalent of the package. Therefore, a $50,000 salary is actually $62,000 in compensation with Employer Y. Needless to say, working for Employer Y will have a much more positive impact on your total earnings than working for Employer X. We'll return to this strategic negotiation point when we examine different salary negotiation strategies in Chapter 8.

4

Know Your Worth and Calculate It Right

WHAT EXACTLY ARE you worth to an employer? Are you a salaried professional who is worth $30,000, $50,000, $75,000, $100,000, or $200,000+ a year or are you a $8.00, $10.00, $15.00, or $25.00 an hour worker? Do you have intrinsic value due to past achievements, or is your value largely determined by the going market rate for someone with your skills? Or perhaps you're only worth what others in similar positions within the organization are paid? Do you know what others make in similar positions and companies? How do pay rates for the same positions vary from one employer to the next, or from one region, state, or city to another?

Valuing Individuals Versus Positions

Knowing what you are worth and what employers are willing to pay for someone with your value are two of the most important yet difficult questions to answer. However, if you don't know your value before applying for a position, you may well apply for the wrong job as well as under-value or over-value yourself.

Let's start by making an important distinction between positions and individuals and then examine the calculations involved in assigning salaries to positions but awarding them to individuals. Employers hire individuals to fill positions within their organizations. They first value the position and then attempt to find individuals with sufficient skills to perform well in the position.

On the other hand, individuals seek positions that offer them maximum value. They are more concerned with their own value than with the value of the position. While both the employer and employee focus their attention on the position, their concepts of what is being valued may differ considerably.

How, then, do employers value positions and their employees? Within every organization you will find a hierarchy of salaries which are assigned to positions. The range between the lowest and highest salaries may be great. Indeed, the lowest paid workers may be hourly custodial and clerical personnel who work for near minimum wage. The top salary may be $500,000 or more, depending on the organization. Expect to see at least a 1 to 25 ratio between the lowest and highest salaries in most organizations with 100 or more employees.

Salary ranges do not differ greatly from one organization to another, although they may appear so to many people who think a few thousand dollars makes a big difference. In general, most entry-level positions will be valued under $30,000 a year, although some hard-to-fill entry-level positions may pay $40,000 or more. Technical and middle management positions will be in the $40,000 to $50,000 range, depending on the level of responsibility. Overall, 80 percent of the employees in most organizations will be making under $50,000 a year.

Calculate the "Going Rate"

While some employers may try to hire personnel at the cheapest rate possible, most employers are more realistic and thus price positions according to the "going rate." Most employers believe labor is a valuable resource which must be hired, rewarded, and nurtured with care regardless of its supply or demand.

The "going rate" is largely determined by internal and external salary comparisons as well as by several current market considerations:

1. **The internal salary structure of the organization.** Salaries will be similar for individuals performing comparable work.

Entry-level salaries for a variety of positions may be very similar.

2. **Salaries for similar positions found in other organizations within the industry as well as the region.** Numerous annual "salary surveys" are conducted for employers who attempt to keep up with salary trends in their industries. Based on this information, employers establish their own salary ranges at, near, or just above the salary ranges offered by the competition or similar types of organizations.

3. **What the market will bear at any particular time given current labor supply and demand considerations.** Salaries will vary depending on what employers are willing to pay given market conditions and the negotiating skills of candidates.

When it comes to salaries, most employers do not want to be pacesetters by offering the highest salaries, nor do they want to be known for being the "cheapest guy in town" by paying the lowest salaries. Most are satisfied with just being "average." Being a little above or below the norm is also quite acceptable. In general, however, the largest and most successful companies tend to pay the best and thus serve as pacesetters for employers in other companies. Few companies ever become successful and productive because they pay cheap wages and exploit their employees.

> *The most successful companies tend to pay the best and thus serve as pacesetters for employers.*

At the same time, most employers prefer making salaries equitable, secret, non-negotiable, and easily administered. They try to keep salaries **equitable** within the organization by not paying anyone much above the internal norm. To do otherwise would appear unfair should others within the organization learn about salary differentials and begin comparing their salaries with those of others who may or may not be as productive. After all, individuals who manage to negotiate higher salaries tend to be those who take initiative concerning their salaries. They get higher salaries because of their negotiating skills and political savvy rather than their increased productivity.

Know Your Worth and Calculate It Right 51

Secrecy is necessary to best deal with the salary inequities that inherently arise due to the nature of the hiring and promotion processes. Without secrecy, considerable internal dissension might ensue should long-term employees discover that a new employee managed to get hired at a much higher salary than employees already working for – and more loyal to – the organization.

Ideally, then, employers prefer keeping salaries **non-negotiable**, because to negotiate with individuals inevitably means creating individual salary inequities as well as uncomfortable employee-employer situations that are best avoided if at all possible. The easiest way to make salaries non-negotiable is to establish a "cut and dry" salary schedule. Companies using such schedules assign specific salary figures to each position and then grade each position for "time in service" salary increments. Developing a salary schedule creates a separate, non-negotiable logic for pay rates. Employees encounter a well-defined salary schedule, established by company policy, which is subject to little or no individual negotiation. Such a salary schedule focuses attention on the value of specific positions rather than on the worth of any one individual.

> *Most employers prefer keeping salaries both equitable and secret.*

The best way for employers to deal with the salary issue is to put into place a pay system that can be **easily administered** to everyone, a system where no special individual compensation agreements exist. If, by chance, salaries become publicized, such a pay system would help minimize the amount of internal conflict because salaries will appear to be equitably assigned and distributed. They will seem fair.

Overall, the tendency toward paying the "norm" is strong amongst most employers. They regularly seek comparative salary information to make sure they are playing the salary game within existing norms. Thinking around the norm is manifested in questions employers ask about salaries. For example, if you ask for a salary higher than the norm, employers will raise objections, which you must respond to, in the form of these two questions:

- But that's much more than others are paid in this industry as well as in our area. Why should we pay you more?

- How can we justify paying you that much when others in our organization with comparable skills and experience are making less?

Going beyond your general desire to get a higher salary because you want it, need it, and feel you deserve it – your obvious need, greed, and self-esteem motivators – how will you respond to these questions with facts about your value that support your request? Your problem, then, is to help the employer break out of this "norm thinking" that is centered around positions rather than focused on you as a unique and exceptional individual who promises to perform above the norm. Therefore, you want to focus on the employer's problems and bottom line rather than on your need, greed, or self-esteem. Your approaches and salary strategies should always be employer-centered rather than self-centered. You must communicate loud and clear to the employer that it is in his or her best interests to pay you what you know you are worth for the position – not your intrinsic ego-driven worth but your worth **in relation to** the employer's position which has already been valued. You must convince the employer that you are worth more than the organization is willing to pay at present.

Focus on the employer's problems and bottom line rather than on your need, greed, or self-esteem.

If the employer wants to attract top talent, then he or she expects to pay above the going rate and beyond the internal norm for the organization. If you want to justify a higher than expected salary, you'll have to convince the employer that you are above the norm in terms of your potential performance – a star performer. On the other hand, for most entry-level positions, salaries offered will be very close to the norm for the companies in the industry and in the same geographic area. Expect little negotiation to take place for such positions unless you show exceptional promise for someone with little or no experience.

While employers know how to price positions, they also have ways of valuing **individuals**. The easiest way of determining what you are worth is to learn what you were paid in your last job. If, for example, last year you made $40,000, in the eyes of most employers you are probably worth no more than an additional 10 to 15 percent – maybe $45,000 a year. If you ask for $60,000 and the employer knows you made only $40,000, he or she may feel you are over-valuing yourself. Depending on what percentage increase you expect over your last salary, it may also be to your advantage to keep your salary history secret!

Most employers know what the going rate is for positions, because they keep in contact with several sources of comparative salary information. The most widely used sources include:

- **Professionals in other organizations who may trade salary information on comparable positions.** They may occasionally ask each other *"By the way, what is your organization paying these days for X, Y, and Z positions? What about benefits?"*

- **Salary surveys of professional associations, executive search firms, and local employment agencies.** If, for example, they are interviewing graduating college seniors for entry-level positions, they may consult the National Association of Colleges and Employers' latest regional salary surveys. Salary information also is readily available on several Internet sites. Try these sites for starters:

    http://jobstar.org
    www.salary.com
    www.payscale.com
    www.monster.com
    www.careerbuilder.com
    www.salaryexpert.com

- **Classified ads in newspapers, magazines, and trade journals which list salaries offered for particular positions and organizations.** Many of these ads will state a specific salary figure or a salary range, depending on the experience of the applicant.

- **Job applicants who state salary requirements.** By interviewing applicants and asking them about their salary history and requirements, employers get first-hand salary information on those they are likely to hire.

Employers also know their internal salary structure as well as yearly cost-of-living increases. What they don't know initially is your past salary history as well as your salary requirements. They need this information in order to determine your value in reference to the value of the position so they can make you what they consider to be both a "reasonable" and "appropriate" salary offer.

Consequently, based on the salary calculations of employers, you are potentially worth the "going rate" plus or minus your present salary and your potential to add value to the organization. Put another way, before you even state your salary requirements, the employer is likely to offer you a salary that reflects two basic elements in his or her salary calculations:

- The value of the position as determined by the employer's various information sources on comparables within and outside the organization.

- Your value as determined by your salary history.

If, for example, you are interviewing for a position valued at $50,000 a year, but your most recent salary was $30,000 a year, you may have difficulty receiving a job offer at the $50,000 level, regardless of how impressive you are on paper as well as in the interview. You simply don't have the salary track record to justify $50,000 a year or more. This employer logic for determining your value is inherently at odds with your own logic that places emphasis on your inherent worth as judged by your performance rather than by others' pay or your salary history.

How, then, do you determine your value and translate it into a salary figure so that you can best communicate your value to employers who, in turn, must translate it into a specific salary offer?

We suggest you follow the same logic as the employer, but add one new element – your **capabilities** as translated into the employer's language of organizational performance. Prior to performing on the job, you must convince the employer that you are a capable individual who will bring additional value to the organization that is above the norm for this and other organizations. In other words, you are an exceptional individual whose talents are worth much more than the average employee. You must be specific here. Can you, for example, demonstrate beyond lofty promises

Know Your Worth and Calculate It Right 55

that your work is likely to generate an additional $300,000 in profits for the organization? By concentrating on your capabilities and potential performance, you **raise** the employer's expectations and thereby create an additional element of value in the salary calculation that goes beyond salary comparables and a salary figure assigned to a position. In so doing, you transcend the position by focusing the salary question on you as an **individual**.

Above all, you need to do research on salaries prior to interviewing for a job. Your research will involve examining salary studies and talking to people with salary information.

> *You must convince the employer that you are a capable individual who will bring additional value to the organization that is above the norm.*

Determine Salary Comparables

With a few exceptions, both you and the employer have access to the same sources of information on salary comparables. The major exception is information on specific salaries within the employer's organization. Such information is usually a closely held secret that only a few well-placed individuals in the organization share with each other in the process of making salary decisions. Since you most likely will not get access to this information, you must guess what this pay system looks like based upon your research of salaries offered by comparable organizations.

Salary Studies and Surveys

Numerous salary surveys are conducted by the government, corporations, associations, employment firms, newspapers, and magazines. While some of these studies are public information, others are confidential studies only available to paying clients. Some of the best and most accessible surveys are found in local libraries, college placement offices, or employment firms.

A good starting point is to consult several books that compile salary information from numerous salary surveys and focus it around discussions of particular occupational fields. One of the most comprehensive such books is the annual *American Salaries and Wages Survey* (Farmington

Hills, MI: Gale Cengage Learning), which includes more than 32,000 salaries for more than 4,500 occupational classifications in thousands of communities throughout the country. This book uses nearly 300 government, business, and news sources for compiling the data.

We also highly recommend acquiring a copy of the *Salary Facts Handbook* (JIST Publishing, 2008), which includes the U.S. Department of Labor pay statistics on 800 jobs.

Other books, such as the U.S. Department of Labor's *Occupational Outlook Handbook* and McGraw-Hill's *Opportunities in...* series, include salary information on hundreds of occupations. These books are widely available in libraries and bookstores. They can also be ordered directly from Impact Publications by completing the order information at the end of this book.

Beyond the books that interpret salary data are the actual salary surveys that present the raw data in statistical tables. The major salary surveys are conducted annually by the following organizations:

- **Department of Labor:** The Bureau of Labor Statistics monitors salaries for numerous occupations nationwide. Its findings are published in several quarterly reports for regions and the nation as a whole: *Industry Wage Surveys, Area Wage Surveys, White-Collar Pay*, and *Employee Benefits Survey*. Another publication, the *Monthly Labor Review* which is the Bureau's monthly journal, regularly summarizes this statistical information. Many libraries have copies of these reports and the journal, or they can be examined in the Bureau of Labor Statistics regional offices which are located in Boston, New York City, Philadelphia, Atlanta, Chicago, Dallas, Kansas City, San Francisco, and Washington, DC.

- **U.S. Office of Personnel Management:** Compiles salary information on government employees at the federal, state, and local levels. The Office of Personnel Management library in Washington, DC will have this information.

- **State and local governments:** Many state and local governments conduct salary and wage surveys for occupations within their geographic area. Contact your state employment commission or county or municipal personnel office to find out if they have such salary information. Your local library should also have information on such surveys. In fact, check with personnel at the information desk, who can quickly access such information. While many of these surveys primarily focus on blue-collar occupations within certain industries, some will also include professional and technical positions. While much of this data may be too generalized by industry to be useful in determining salary ranges for particular positions, it will give you some idea of average salaries paid in your particular geographic area.

- **Executive search, employment, and consulting firms:** Many executive search, employment, and consulting firms conduct their own salary surveys of selected occupations. Some firms are commissioned to do these surveys for corporate clients whereas others compile this information for advertising and public relations purposes. For example, Robert Half International, a staffing services firm with over 400 offices in North America, Latin America, Europe, Asia, Australia, and New Zealand, each year publishes a series of five salary survey booklets for positions in finance, accounting, law, creative fields, and administration. You can request free copies of these reports by contacting Robert Half (www.rhii.com). Other noted firms conducting salary studies include The Economic Research Institute (www.erieri.com), Source Services, and Abbott, Langer, and Associates (see Chapter 12). While most of these studies are conducted for clients, some are also sold to the public. While expensive to acquire, some of the salary information appearing in these studies appear in major magazines and newspapers, such as *Money Magazine* and *The Wall Street Journal.*

- **Trade and professional associations:** One of the best and most reliable sources for salary information by occupation and geographic area are the more than 3,000 trade and professional associations that are primarily headquartered in Washington, DC, New York City, and Chicago. Most of these associations conduct an annual salary survey of their members. Usually published in one issue of their newsletter or magazine, the survey identifies who makes how much and where. The National

Association of Broadcasters, for example, publishes an annual compensation and fringe benefit report that outlines the average salaries of its members. The American Association of University Professors publishes an annual salary survey for higher education. The American Federation of Teachers as well as the National Education Association publish similar surveys for elementary and secondary teachers. If you are interested in salaries for engineers, contact the National Society of Professional Engineers which also conducts its own annual salary survey. If you are interested in surveying entry-level salaries offered by the major college recruiters, you should examine the National Association of Colleges and Employers' quarterly and annual *Salary Survey* which is available in many college and university offices of career planning and placement. If you are not familiar with these associations, the best places to start are **Associations on the Internet** (www.ipl.org/div/aon) and three useful directories found in the reference section of most libraries: *The Encyclopedia of Associations* (Farmington Hills, MI: Gale Cengage Learning), *National Trade and Professional Associations* (Washington, DC: Columbia Books), and *Associations USA* (Detroit: Omnigraphics). Revised annually, these directories provide contact information and summaries on more than 20,000 domestic and international associations. If you can't find an association relevant to your particular occupation in these three directories, you can safely assume that no such association exists. Once you locate an appropriate association, call their main office and ask if they have information on salary ranges for your particular occupational specialty and geographic area.

- **Journals and magazines:** Numerous journals and magazines also conduct salary studies as well as publicize the survey findings of other organizations. *Adweek*, for example, publishes an annual salary survey for the advertising field. *Fortune* and *Inc.* magazines usually reveal the salaries of CEOs in Fortune 500 companies. The *Public Relations Journal* publishes salaries of public relations professionals. The *Compensation Review* keeps compensation specialists informed on salaries and benefits within their industries.

- **Newspapers:** Some newspapers will occasionally conduct their own salary surveys among industries within their community. Others report the survey findings of various salary studies.

Classified Ads and Job Listings

Two of the most important sources for salary information are the classified sections of newspapers, magazines, trade journals, and newsletters and job listings available through employment offices. Many employment ads will reveal the salaries or salary ranges being offered for particular positions. By periodically surveying these ads, you may get a fairly accurate idea of who is paying what in your geographic area.

Employment offices, both public and private, are repositories for job vacancy announcements and other information on salaries. Employers listing with these offices normally include the salary ranges for each position announced.

However, don't expect to find salaries listed for all types of positions. Salaries for blue-collar and hourly positions will most often appear in classified ads and in employment offices. While some ads and vacancy announcements may list the salaries for higher level professional and technical positions, many do not. Invariably they will include general statements such as *"salary and benefits commensurate with qualifications and experience"* or *"we offer a competitive salary and an excellent fringe benefit package."* Alternatively, the ad may request that you submit your salary history, salary requirements, or salary expectations along with your resume when applying for the position. These statements and instructions, in effect, notify you that there is flexibility with the salary and thus it is negotiable within certain limits as determined by both the employer and your salary history.

One of the best sources for salary information on professional and technical positions are the classified sections of major newspapers. For example, the Sunday editions of *The New York Times, Washington Post,* and the *Los Angeles Times* will include extensive listings of professional and technical positions. If you survey a few issues of these newspapers, you should be able to get a sense of what employers are offering for the type of position you are seeking – at least in those specific metropolitan areas. Many of these classified ads are now available on various websites.

Be sure to survey your own local newspaper and related publications. While newspapers in major metropolitan areas will provide you with salary information for positions in major cities, many of these advertisements may reflect salaries that are 20 to 30 percent higher than in most other communities. Therefore, the classified ads appearing in your local newspaper should more accurately reflect the pricing of jobs in your community. Survey these major national publications, but also know what is being offered locally.

Special Reports and Projects

You may also discover special reports and projects that include information on salaries. Faculty and research offices at your local college and university may regularly conduct salary surveys and publish their results in reports that have limited distribution beyond their immediate institution. You may also discover special job search projects that include information on salaries. For example, in our own state of Virginia, a computerized job search program called *Virginia View* includes information on salary ranges both within Virginia and nationwide for numerous types of positions: www.vaview.vt.edu. Centered at Virginia Tech University in Blacksburg, Virginia, this program is available throughout the state at most college and university career planning and placement offices as well as in many local libraries and state employment offices. The project also includes a toll-free Career Information Hotline number for state residents in need of job and career assistance: 800-542-5870. You may find similar types of projects operating in your state or local community. Contact your local library, state employment office, or college and university career planning and placement office for information on any such special reports and projects.

Networking for Information

The final source of information for salaries and salary ranges for determining your value will be your own networking activities. Indeed, this may well become the best and most reliable source of information on salaries that most directly relates to the type of position you are seeking.

Networking plays a central role in any well organized and targeted job search. It involves the process of contacting individuals for information, advice, and referrals in reference to your job search. It encompasses a specific set of targeted activities that will eventually yield nonadvertised job opportunities. Your networking might include talking to relatives, neighbors, friends, colleagues, and acquaintances or making new contacts with strangers, including employment specialists and potential employers who have information on the types of jobs you are seeking. While you will want to gather a great deal of word-of-mouth information from these people on job vacancies, qualifications, responsibilities, work environments, and advancement opportunities, you also want to ask questions about salaries and compensation packages. For example, as part of your informational interviewing activities, you should pose one of two simple nonthreatening salary research questions:

What is the normal salary range for this type of job?

or

What do individuals with these qualifications and levels of responsibility normally make in this industry? And what are the fringe benefits that normally come with this job?

As we will see later, these are the same types of questions you may want to ask an interviewer if he or she raises the issue of salary early on in the interview. This question will quickly yield salary information from individuals who know exactly what is being paid for the type of job that most interests you. When conducting informational interviews for networking purposes, under no circumstances should you ask the person you are interviewing about their salary. People are much more willing to reveal salary information on others than on themselves. They consider such a directed question an invasion of their privacy. Therefore, make sure you direct the salary question away from the individual as you attempt to determine the value of jobs and positions rather than the person you are interviewing.

People are much more willing to reveal salary information on others than on themselves.

The networking process and the methodology for conducting the informational interview are outlined in detail in two of our other books: **You Should Hire Me!** and **The Savvy Networker** (Impact Publications).

Conduct Your Own Salary Survey

The most productive way to determine the value of positions, as well as your own value, is to conduct your own salary survey. This involves a five-step procedure for gathering salary information on the positions and organizations that most interest you.

1. **Read literature on jobs and salary ranges.** Recommended readings include *American Salaries and Wages Survey, Salary Facts Handbook, The Occupational Outlook Handbook,* and numerous salary reports issued by the U.S. Department of Labor's Bureau of Labor Statistics. Many of these salary reports are summarized in the Bureau of Labor Statistics's journal, the *Monthly Labor Review.* All of these resources should be available in your local library.

2. **Visit your local library for information.** Local libraries and librarians are precious resources for conducting a job search as well as for gathering comparative salary information. If you are not an expert on library resources, it's best to approach the information desk or someone in the reference section and ask them about resources on salary ranges. Experienced librarians are wonderful sources for all types of information. Tell them exactly what you are doing and let them solve your problem by directing you to their resources. For example, approach them in the following manner:

   I'm in the process of gathering information on salaries for jobs in _____. What might be some good information sources you could recommend? For example, do you have the salary survey reports of the Bureau of Labor Statistics or similar surveys conducted by state and local government agencies? Do you know of anyone who might have this information?

   You may be surprised by the wealth of information and cooperation this question generates! In addition to directing you to the appropriate in-house resources, the librarian may suggest individuals and organizations you might include in your networking activities, such as a local employment agency, executive search firm, or consulting firm that gathers salary information. You should also consult the standard reference indexes that will give you access to hundreds of journals, magazines, newspapers, newsletters, and reports relevant to jobs and salaries: *Readers' Guide to Periodical Literature, Standard Periodical Directory,* and *Business Periodicals Index.* Many libraries also have computerized reference systems that enable you to quickly research numerous journals, magazines, and newspapers for articles on jobs and salaries. If you've not used these systems before, this is a good time and place to quickly learn what is a basic and essential research tool for gathering this type of information. A little time and effort in learning how to use these resources will more than pay for itself when it comes time to negotiate salary, and you have the information necessary to strike the best deal possible.

3. **Contact professional associations and employment specialists.** Most professional associations and numerous employment firms conduct yearly salary surveys. Again, www.ipl.org/div/aon and your local library should have the key directories – *Encyclopedia of Associations, National Trade and Professional Associations,* and *Associations USA* – which provide contact information on all major associations. They should also have directories to employment and executive search firms that might have salary survey information.

4. **Explore Internet sites that offer salary information:** Numerous websites now offer information on salaries. Many sites include salary calculators as well as post job listings that include salary information. Explore a few of these popular sites for starters:

Monster.com	www.monster.com
Careerbuilder.com	www.careerbuilder.com
JobCentral	www.jobcentral.com
NationJob	www.nationjob.com
FlipDog	www.flipdog.com

Hot Jobs	http://hotjobs.yahoo.com
CareerJournal	http://online.wsj.com/careers

5. **Talk to people in your expanding network.** Once you have gathered preliminary salary information from published sources, talk to people who have information on salary ranges for the types of jobs that interest you. This involves the process of networking for information, advice, and referrals. One of the best approaches is to conduct a research project on salary ranges by telephoning personnel offices and asking for assistance with your research. Begin by mentioning that you are conducting research on salary ranges and would appreciate their assistance. In exchange for their cooperation, tell them *"I'll share my research findings with you."* Since many personnel offices are interested in current comparative salary information, they may be happy to share this information with you. If you conclude your telephone interview with the referral question *"Whom else would you suggest I contact for similar information?,"* you should receive additional names and telephone numbers of people who are "in the know" about the salaries that interest you. Within a few hours, you should have a good idea of current salary ranges. But be sure to call back or write a nice thank-you letter in which you share your research findings with your informants. Not only is this the proper thing to do, it provides these people with useful information for their own decision-making. Another approach is to call employment offices, executive search firms, headhunters, career planning offices, and career counselors and ask them if they have any information on such salaries or if they can recommend anyone who might. While these are secondary sources since they are one or two steps removed from the personnel offices who have the most accurate information, many of these informants will have a fairly accurate picture of current salary ranges. A final approach, which we discussed earlier, involves asking about salaries during your informational interviews. An advantage of these sources is that you get salary information applicable to your geographical area.

6. **Set a dollar figure on your value:** While you arrive at a realistic market value figure by examining comparative salary information, you may also want to set an arbitrary salary figure that you believe you are worth. This arbitrary decision may help guide you toward acquiring new skills and seeking higher level jobs.

Document Your Performance

If you verbally emphasize the importance of performance in determining compensation, you must first document your performance – create a portfolio of performance which includes examples of your achievements. Documentation gives you the necessary **supports** for justifying what you're worth.

You should document both your past and present performance by keeping records on your achievements. Your past achievements should be documented as part of your self-assessment – one of the first things you should have done in your job search. If you did not complete this critical step at that time, better late than never. One of best ways to do this is to complete the form on page 66. Make at least 10 copies of this form. Complete the questions for each of 10 major achievements related to your previous work. This exercise helps you identify your **motivated abilities**, which are also your **strengths**. When focusing on achievements relevant to particular jobs and employers, your motivated abilities and strengths become your **performance**. By addressing the questions on this form, you detail each of your achievements around employer's major concerns. If, for example, an employer asks you during the interview *"What are your major strengths?,"* you will be prepared to detail at least 10 strengths that also explain your past performance. You should do more than just list 10 discrete activities you engaged in that demonstrate some degree of performance. Indeed, if you go one step further and synthesize all of these achievements into two or three common strengths, you should be able to communicate a picture of past performance that also constitutes a **pattern** for predicting future performance. Much of the information you generate from this exercise should also appear on your resume.

Your Achievements

INSTRUCTIONS: Prioritize what you believe are your most important achievements in your worklife. An achievement is anything you enjoyed doing, felt you did well, developed a sense of satisfaction, accomplishment, and pride in doing. Make 10 copies of this form and complete one form for each achievement. Focus on only the achievements that relate to previous jobs and employers.

ACHIEVEMENT # ___: _____

_____

1. How did I get involved? _____

_____

_____

2. What did I do? _____

_____

_____

3. How did I do it? _____

_____

_____

4. What did I especially enjoy about doing it? _____

_____

_____

5. Who benefitted how from what I did? _____

_____

_____

6. How was I recognized and rewarded? _____

_____

_____

_____

You should also document your present performance as well as prepare to continue doing so in the future by keeping records of your accomplishments. While you and your employer may complete a standardized performance appraisal form for this purpose, you should go one step further in keeping a **performance diary** that details your accomplishments. Again, avoid the tendency to merely list duties and responsibilities that are on-going activities related to your job. You want to emphasize **outcomes** and **benefits** from your performance. Include the following categories of information in your performance diary:

1. Date: _____

2. What did I accomplish? _____
   _____
   _____
   _____

3. Who was involved? _____
   _____
   _____
   _____

4. Who or what benefited from what I did? _____
   _____
   _____
   _____

5. How did I communicate this accomplishment to my supervisor? _____
   _____
   _____
   _____

Calculate Your Value and Your Salary Range

Once you know the average salary range for a position, you can calculate a rough estimate of your value for a position. Use the following formula for computing your value:

1. The average salary or mid-point of the
   salary range for the position (this figure
   is based on your research): $ _____

2. Your most recent or present salary: $ _____

3. Subtotal (add the two figures and
   divide by 2): $ _____

4. Multiple by 15% (.15 x the figure
   in Item 3): $ _____

5. Add Items 3 and 4; this is your estimated
   value for the position: $ _____

6. Salary range: calculate plus and
   minus 15% of the figure in Item 5: $ _____ to $ _____

If, for example, you know the salary range for the position is $40,000 to $55,000 (average is $47,500) and your current salary is $42,000 per year, based on this formula, your estimated value for this position should be $51,463. Your salary range (Item 6) for the position would be $43,744 to $59,182. You should focus your base pay negotiations toward the top end of this range – $55,000 to $59,000.

By calculating salary in this manner, you should be able to get a clear picture of your current market value. Furthermore, your calculations should be similar to those of the employer. One important result of this exercise should be reaching some common statistical ground from which to negotiate your salary. At the same time, you must factor in the value of your past achievements. Were you adequately compensated for the level of your performance? If not, perhaps you need to increase your multiple in Item 4 by 10 percent – from 15 percent to 25 percent. Unless you especially dislike your present job, a move to another job should result in at least a 15 percent increase in salary.

Be Prepared

Whatever you do, make sure you know what both the position and you are worth. One of the best ways to kill your financial future is by being both unprepared and unrealistic about your future salary when asked about your "salary requirements" or "salary expectations."

If you conduct your own salary survey as suggested in this chapter, you will quickly be on the road to salary success. You will be prepared to clearly communicate to employers that you are worth a salary commensurate with your salary expectations. You'll be able to address the two key salary considerations of the employer – the value of the position both within and outside the organization and your salary history – as well as focus on what should become the most important ingredient in the salary calculation – your potential performance in adding value to the employer's organization and operations.

One of the best ways to kill your financial future is by being both unprepared and unrealistic about your future salary.

5

30 Rules for Success

WHY ARE SOME PEOPLE more successful in finding jobs and negotiating higher salaries than others? Are they more intelligent or talented than other people? Do they know something about the job search and how to approach employers that others don't? What is it they do that enables them to achieve their salary goals to a much greater extent than others?

Learn and Follow the Rules

Over the years we have learned that successful people do indeed do things differently from others. They're not necessarily more intelligent nor more talented than others. But they are smart in how they approach situations and work with people. They especially know how to deal with the salary issue.

If you want to be successful at both finding a job and achieving your salary goals, you must orient yourself to success. This means taking certain actions that result in clearly communicating your value to employers. Above all, it means following certain rules for job search and salary success. These rules constitute a set of principles for conducting dynamite salary negotiations.

Orient Yourself to Job Search Success

Job search success is determined by more than just a good plan getting implemented. It is not predetermined, nor is it primarily achieved by intelligence, thinking big, time management, or luck. Based upon experience, theory, research, and common sense, we believe you will achieve job search success by following many of these 21 principles:

1. **You should work hard at finding a job:** Make this a daily endeavor and involve your family. Spend the necessary time conducting research on organizations offering job opportunities as well as networking amongst those that are of most interest to you.

2. **You should not be discouraged by setbacks:** You are playing the odds, so expect disappointments and handle them in stride. You will get many "no's" before finding the one "yes" which is right for you. If you are unable to deal with rejections as part of the game, you will be headed for trouble. Try to turn negatives into positives. Learn from them, leave them, but remember them as stepping stones to future acceptances.

3. **You should be patient and persevere:** Expect three to six months of hard work before you connect with the job that's right for you.

4. **You should be honest with yourself and others:** Honesty is always the best policy. But don't be naive by confessing your negatives and shortcomings to others.

5. **You should develop a positive attitude toward yourself:** Nobody wants to employ guilt-ridden people with inferiority complexes. At the same time, neither do they want to hire self-centered individuals. Focus on your positive characteristics as well as the employer's needs.

6. **You should associate with positive and successful people:** Finding a job largely depends on how well you relate to others and how effectively you network within the job market. Avoid

associating with negative and depressing people who complain and have a "you-can't-do-it" attitude. Run with winners who have a positive "can-do" outlook on life.

7. **You should set goals:** You should have a clear idea of what you want and where you are going. Without these, you will present a confusing and indecisive image to others. Clear goals help direct your job search into productive channels. Moreover, setting high goals also will help make you work hard in getting what you want.

8. **You should plan:** Convert your goals into action steps that are organized as short, intermediate, and long-range plans. You should operationalize these plans so they can be realistically implemented.

9. **You should get organized:** Translate your plans into activities, targets, names, addresses, telephone numbers, and materials. Develop an efficient and effective filing system and use a large calendar to set time targets, record appointments, and compile useful information.

10. **You should be a good communicator:** Take stock of your oral, written, and nonverbal communication skills. How well do you communicate? Since most aspects of your job search involve communicating with others, and communication skills are one of the most sought-after skills, always present yourself well both verbally and nonverbally.

11. **You should be energetic and enthusiastic:** Employers are attracted to positive people. They don't like negative and depressing people who toil at their work. Generate enthusiasm both verbally and nonverbally. Check on your telephone voice – it may be less enthusiastic than your voice in face-to-face situations.

12. **You should ask questions:** Your best information comes from asking questions. Learn to develop intelligent questions that are non-aggressive, polite, and interesting to others. But don't ask too many questions and thereby become a bore.

13. **You should be a good listener:** Being a good listener is often more important than being a good questioner or talker. Learn to improve your face-to-face listening behavior (nonverbal cues) as well as remember and use information gained from others. Make others feel they enjoy talking with you – you are one of the few people who actually **listens** to what they say.

14. **You should be polite, courteous, and thoughtful:** Treat gatekeepers, especially receptionists and secretaries, with respect. Avoid being aggressive or too assertive. Try to be polite, courteous, and gracious. Your social graces are being observed. Remember to send thank-you letters – a very thoughtful thing to do in a job search. Even if rejected, thank employers for the "opportunity" given to you. After all, they may later have additional opportunities, and they may remember you. Thank-you letters get remembered by employers.

15. **You should be tactful:** Watch what you say to others about other people and your background. Don't be a gossip or backstabber.

16. **You should maintain a professional stance:** Be neat in what you do and wear, and speak with the confidence, authority, and maturity of a professional.

17. **You should demonstrate your intelligence and competence:** Present yourself as someone who gets things done and achieves results – a **producer**. Employers generally seek people who are bright, hard working, responsible, can communicate well, have positive personalities, maintain good interpersonal relations, are likable, observe dress and social codes, take initiative, are talented, possess expertise in particular areas, use good judgment, are cooperative, trustworthy, and loyal, generate confidence and credibility, and are conventional. In other words, they like people who score in the "excellent" to "outstanding" categories of the annual performance evaluation.

18. **You should maximize your contacts through networking:** Interpersonal networking still remains the key to getting the right

job. It's not something you turn on and off when you need something from others – that's using others, not networking. You need to constantly renew old contacts, manage current contacts, and develop new contacts for maintaining and expanding your network of personal and professional contacts. These contacts will serve you well in your quests for finding a job, changing careers, or advancing on the job.

19. **You should not overdo your job search:** Don't engage in overkill and bore everyone with your "job search" stories. Achieve balance in everything you do. Occasionally take a few days off to do nothing related to your job search. Develop a system of incentives and rewards – such as two free days a week if you accomplish targets A, B, C, and D.

20. **You should be open-minded and keep an eye open for "luck":** Too much planning can blind you to unexpected and fruitful opportunities. You should welcome serendipity. Learn to re-evaluate your goals and strategies. Seize new opportunities if they appear appropriate.

21. **You should evaluate your progress and adjust:** Take two hours once every two weeks and evaluate what you are doing and accomplishing. If necessary, tinker with your plans and reorganize your activities and priorities. Don't become too routinized and thus kill creativity and innovation.

While these 21 principles specifically apply to organizing and implementing a job search that leads to a job offer, these principles are equally valid for individuals who are negotiating salary as part of the job offer, approaching an employer for a raise, or renegotiating the terms of employment.

Nine additional principles are more directly applicable to salary negotiations:

1. Value yourself appropriately
2. Document your value
3. Use supports
4. Project an image of value and success

30 Rules for Success

5. Invest the employer's time in you
6. Ask and answer questions intelligently
7. Take notes during negotiations
8. Be realistic and seek common ground
9. Be thoughtful and mindful of the future

Let's examine each of these principles as it pertains to negotiating salaries. In so doing, you should be armed with 30 principles for conducting a dynamite job search that leads to the right job and a dynamite salary.

Value Yourself Appropriately

Knowing what you are worth and communicating it to employers can be difficult if you price yourself too high or too low. If you are too high, employers may view you as either unrealistic or over-qualified given the structure of their compensation system. On the other hand, you can price yourself too low and thus communicate that you have little value; you are probably under-qualified for the job. The notion that pricing yourself low will give you a better chance at getting and keeping a job is largely a myth. If you under-value yourself, you may not receive the respect you need in order to do a good job. You can give yourself additional value in the eyes of many employers if you price yourself above the norm – but not too much above it.

> *You can price yourself too low and thus communicate that you have little value.*

Document Your Value

Negotiating techniques are only as good as the information you bring to the negotiations. You will need to justify why you feel you are worth what you say you are worth. More importantly, you must address any objections employers may have to paying you more than what they feel you are worth as well as the amount already budgeted for the position. The best way to do this is to document your achievements and communicate your past achievements as strong indicators of your future performance which will be above the norm. This involves carefully going through the process of knowing what you are worth as outlined in Chapter 4. You might reformulate your documentation into a checklist of *"10 Reasons Why I Should Be Given a Salary of $ _____ a Year."*

Use Supports

When you make statements about your accomplishments and productivity, try to back them up with **supports**. While documentation is the basis for developing supports (Chapter 4), supports come in many different forms and involve several techniques of persuasion. Can you give an **example** of how you improved production on your last job? Can you **describe** the sales campaign that won you the Best-Copywriter-of-the-Year Award? Can you **compare** the previous bookkeeping system with the one you instituted that saved your last or present employer so much money? When you back up your assertions with supports, you gain several advantages over individuals who do not. Supports help clarify your comments, help substantiate them, help the listener recall them at a later time, and they add interest. You should use a variety of supports in the process of persuading the employer that you are indeed worth what you say you are. Supports include:

> *Always project an image of success that is equivalent to your expected value.*

- examples
- illustrations
- descriptions
- statistics
- comparisons
- testimonials
- definitions
- stories

Use such supports in stressing your accomplishments, which are the basis for communicating your value to employers.

Project an Image of Value and Success

Whether you are conducting a job search or performing on the job, always project an image of success that is equivalent to your expected value. During the job search, your image is projected in your resumes, letters, application forms, networking activities, informational interviews, and job interviews. You must write first-class resumes and letters. When networking and interviewing, you must dress appropriately for the type of position you are seeking. Your use of language and the types of questions you ask must communicate your value.

People who command high salaries tend to communicate an **image of class** which is expressed in the quality of their apparel, grooming, nonverbal behaviors, questions, answers, speech, and follow-up behavior. Indeed, your nonverbal behaviors may be more important in justifying your salary requirements than what you say in a salary negotiation session. If you are renegotiating your compensation with your present employer, it's especially important that you have been continuously projecting an image of value and success while on the job.

Invest the Employer's Time in You

The use of time is very important when negotiating salary. Try to invest as much of the employer's time in you as possible. You will have value to the employer as you use up more of his or her time. The best way to do this is to keep the salary question to the very end of the job interview(s). However, should the employer raise the question of salary at the beginning of the application process or during the initial job interview, try to keep your response to the very last job interview. You do this by saying something to this effect:

> *I'm open at present. But I really need to know more about this position and your organization as well as what others with my qualifications normally make. If you don't mind, I'd prefer discussing this matter later, after we've had a chance to address several important questions about the job and how I might best fit into your organization.*

Indeed, the whole purpose of the application process and a series of job interviews should be to exchange information about the value of both the job and you. You want to communicate your value to the employer **before** finally translating your value into a specific salary figure. The employer does not know your value until after he or she has invested time in getting answers to several questions about your achievements and performance. Answers to these questions are not found in resumes, letters, and application forms. Therefore, the answer to the salary question should ideally take place at the very **end** of your last interview, just prior to being offered the job or accepting it contingent upon reaching agreement on compensation.

Ask and Answer Questions Intelligently

You must be prepared to give positive answers and ask intelligent questions relevant to compensation. Most employers will ask you about your salary history and salary requirements. If your past salaries were low in comparison to the position in question, you will need to explain why you should be compensated at a much higher rate than in your last position. If your salary requirements are much higher than expected, the employer is likely to object to paying you above the range set for the position. Thus, you will need to respond to the two most common objections:

That's more than others with similar qualifications and experience make.

We're not budgeted to pay that much.

At the same time, you need to ask intelligent questions about the position, company, and employer that will help you make the best decisions possible. For example, what type of pay system operates within this organization? Is compensation tied to performance criteria? If so, what exactly is the criteria and how is it uniformly applied to employees? Does an annual performance appraisal determine pay increases, and how does it operate in practice? What have been the average annual salary increments during the past five years, especially for the position you are considering? Are these primarily cost-of-living increases? What about such benefits as health insurance, child care, education and training, and retirement? How are they structured? How much do employees contribute to the plans? In other words, you should talk about the **details** of compensation rather than deal with salary and benefits in general terms. After all, it's the details that will give you problems once you accept a position and discover that the so-called attractive compensation looked most attractive on paper rather than in practice. In the process of doing so, you again demonstrate your value to employers who, in turn, will respect you more for your knowledge of the employment process.

Take Notes During Negotiations

While it is best to memorize your main points concerning compensation, it's not always possible to remember everything you need to at such an important meeting. Feel free to take notes during the negotiation session as well as bring notes with you that outline issues and questions you need to address with the employer. Especially when you address the question of benefits, it's a good idea to have a checklist of the various types of benefits you expect and notes about the details on each benefit. While some employers may not have answers to each of these questions, by preparing in this manner you at least impress upon the employer that the content of the compensation package is important to you, that you want to be rewarded for performance, and that compensation will be an ongoing issue with you rather than something that is only settled at the job offer stage. Again, you increase your value in the eyes of most employers by approaching the salary negotiations in such a manner.

Be Realistic and Seek Common Ground

You want to approach the question of compensation from the employer's perspective rather than from one of need, greed, or gamesmanship. Keep in mind that most employers have problems they need to solve by hiring new employees. Paying an employee a few hundred or thousand dollars more than expected is really not a major problem for most employers, if they know they will get better value for their money. However, keep in mind that some employers have little flexibility with their pay systems which are often rigidly structured around base pay. You need to sense whether the employer has more flexibility with salary or benefits and negotiate accordingly.

> *Approach the question of compensation from the employer's perspective rather than from one of need, greed, or gamesmanship.*

Conventional wisdom suggests that benefits are generally standard and hence one should concentrate on negotiating salary. But in some instances, salary may be fixed – or at least a ceiling on salary for the position is in place. In these situations, there may be some leeway on the benefits side. For example, we know individuals in education administration – an area where there are caps on salary ranges – knowing they were being offered the top dollar amount which the university could pay for their job slot, who bargained for two days off each month during which they could do consulting. At $500 a day, that's an additional $12,000 a year!

Being realistic means knowing what both you and the position are worth and then reaching common ground with the employer on the question of compensation. Needy people often say "yes" to the initial offer just to get the job and avoid any stressful questions about money. Greedy people often over-estimate their worth by playing a game that no one else sees value in continuing, or winning a game in which they may eventually become the loser. Indeed, many employees over-value themselves by thinking they are indispensable to employers and threaten to quit unless their salary demands. Not surprisingly, they are often shown the door as a measure of their true value to employers who know that most employees are replaceable – and often at lower compensation.

> Being realistic means knowing what both you and the position are worth and then reaching common ground with the employer.

The fastest way to eliminate yourself from consideration or initially create problems on the job is to get greedy during the salary stage and thereby force the employer into making a decision he or she feels uncomfortable about but makes nonetheless in order to get the troublesome hiring process over. Your clever negotiation skills may create ill will at this crucial juncture of the hiring process. If you leave with a job offer from an employer who does not feel good about acceding to your demands, he or she may keep you under close scrutiny in an effort to justify paying your high price.

A general rule is to know when to stop negotiating and start the job. Reaching common ground and setting the stage for mutual respect and cooperation are more important than the few extra dollars you might be able to wring out of the employer by playing hardball when negotiating salary.

Be Thoughtful and Mindful of the Future

Every step in the interview process should be focused on setting the stage for being a respected employee. How well you perform in the interview, as well as negotiate your salary, will affect how well you get along on the job. Few employers desire adversarial relationships with their employees. While the employer-employee relationship is instrumental in some respects – your talent in exchange for money – on the other hand, this relationship also involves mutual respect and admiration. Therefore, you should also develop good personal relations with your employer that go beyond the instrumental monetary bonds that hold you together.

One of the best ways to begin developing this personal relationship is to be thoughtful during the interview and salary negotiation stages by sending thank-you letters. Within 48 hours of completing your first interview, send a nice thank-you letter in which you express your appreciation for the opportunity to interview for the position and stress your continuing interest in the position. An example of such a letter appears in Chapter 9.

After you receive a firm job offer with the question of compensation settled, send an acceptance thank-you letter in which you reiterate your interest in working with the employer and contributing to the success of his or her operations. This thank-you letter is a thoughtful thing to do that very few new employees ever do. In addition, it helps relieve doubts that employers may have about hiring you. Best of all, most employers **remember** such thoughtful gestures as they begin developing both personal and professional relationships with their new employees. Such a letter expresses an important **attitude** toward the employer and the job that is of central concern to most employers as they scrutinize new employees during the first 90 days. It's always best to be initially remembered as a thoughtful person rather than just another new employee who will be tested in the months ahead.

Additional Resources for Salary Success

Much of salary success is a function of attitude, motivation, and persistence. For more information on the principles of success, we recommend the following inspirational books, which are available through Impact Publications (see the order form at the end of this book as well as visit the online bookstore, www.impactpublications.com):

7 Habits of Highly Effective People (Stephen R. Covey)
The 8th Habit (Stephen R. Covey)
100 Ways to Motivate Yourself (Steve Chandler)
Attitude Is Everything (Keith Harrell)
Awaken the Giant Within (Anthony Robbins)
Change Your Thinking, Change Your Life (Brian Tracy)
Dream It, Do It (Sharon Cook and Graciela Sholander)
Flight Plan: The Real Secret to Success (Brian Tracy)
Goals! (Brian Tracy)
Little Gold Book of YES! Attitudes (Jeffrey Gitomer)
Little Green Book of Getting Your Way (Jeffrey Gitomer)
The Secret (Rhonda Byrne, editor)
The Success Principles (Jack Canfield)
The Power of Positive Thinking (Keith Harrell)
Think Big (Dr. Ben Carson and Cecil Murphy)

6

Respond Right to Ads and Applications

THE QUESTION OF SALARY is likely to arise during two different stages of the job search: at the beginning, when completing an application; and toward the end, when interviewing for the job and negotiating the job offer. It can also arise anytime during your job search. Whenever it does become an issue, you need to respond in a manner that is most advantageous to your financial future.

Handling the Compensation Issue

Your response to the compensation issue will take different forms. For example, at the application stage you must be prepared to identify in writing both your salary history and salary requirements – your financial past and expected future. During the job interview you may address the same issues, but this time you will do so in reference to your demonstrated value and to the employer's position, pay system, and opportunities for advancement.

How you handle the compensation question at each stage will largely determine if you will proceed to the next stage and eventually receive a firm job offer. The job offer, which includes a compensation package, is the final stage of your job search. This is the point where you should negotiate salary and terms of employment in earnest.

Salary Issues

Let's do first things first. At the very beginning of a job search you must be prepared to deal with four salary-related situations which are most likely to arise prior to a job interview. These include:

1. Determining the value of jobs in terms of specific salary and benefits.

2. Dealing with requests for information about your salary history.

3. Stating your salary requirements.

4. Responding to vacancy announcements which identify salary for specific positions.

Each of these situations requires thoughtful responses that should result in leaving the door open for a series of job interviews that eventually lead to a job offer which specifies a compensation package. For example, when you read a vacancy announcement that does not mention salary, how will you know if the position fits within your expected salary range? What can you do to determine the value of the position prior to spending your time applying for what may appear to be a $50,000 a year job but in reality is nothing more than a well written ad for a $25,000 a year job?

At the same time, how will you respond to an ad or an application that asks you to reveal either your salary history or your salary expectations? Will you state a specific figure that might be too high or too low and thus eliminate you from further consideration, or should you disregard this request altogether? And what will you do if you find an ad for a job that states a salary range that may appear too high or too low given your present salary? Should you disregard this job altogether, because it may be above or beneath your qualifications and experience, or should you pursue it nonetheless?

Let's address these questions **before** you get that first telephone call that turns into a screening interview which may lead to the first of two or three job interviews, and a job offer where the question of compensation arises again. For, in addressing the salary question at this initial application stage, you will be better prepared to deal with it over the telephone and in face-to-face interview settings.

Determine the Value of Jobs

If you browse through the business and classified sections of most Saturday or Sunday newspapers, you will discover hundreds of job listings. Some state a specific salary or salary range whereas others only give information about the job and how to apply. Take, for example, the following three ads which appeared in nationwide publications:

TREASURER

Dynamic individual with proven history and ability in real estate and equipment financing, as well as cash management, needed for newly created position. The privately held XXXX group of affiliated companies specialize in both truckload transportation as well as commercial real estate. Send resume and salary requirements in strict confidence to: (mailing address)

HUMAN RESOURCES ASSISTANT

XXXX Group is a dynamic company offering a variety of financial services. We are currently seeking an individual to fill this position in our human resources department. Individual will be responsible for processing employee status changes, enrolling and administering benefits plans, chairing compensation committee and coordinating updates of company administration plans. Qualified applicant must have 1-2 years experience in a human resources environment, strong communication skills. Prior experience or education in compensation and benefits administration strongly desired. Excellent benefits package including dental/vision and free parking. Please send resume with salary history to: (mailing address)

RESEARCH ANALYST

The Marketing Services Department of a prestigious National Trade Association seeks individual to perform analysis and research of electronic industries. Position requires a degree in business or economics with course work in statistics and at least one year applicable experience. Candidates must be highly organized, detail oriented and have strong quantitative and communication skills. Knowledge of Lotus, Harvard Graphics, and WordPerfect desired. Overtime necessary. This is a non-smoking office. Salary to low $30's with excellent benefits. Send resume with salary requirements to: (mailing address)

While you can easily screen in or out those jobs which mention salary, other jobs are somewhat of a mystery. Indeed, many ads may sound like a job pays $60,000 or more, but in reality someone did a great job writing an attractive ad for a $25,000 a year job. How much, for example, do you think this job pays?

> **WAREHOUSE/PRODUCTION**
>
> Hardworking individuals needed for quality fabrication/production work. Training provided. Good references necessary. Must be willing to work 40 to 50 hours per week. Only those interested in a career opportunity please apply in person to: (address)

This job actually pays $9.50 an hour or $380 per week.

Want ads and vacancy announcements that do not provide information on salaries can be a waste of your time and effort. In some cases an employer is just "testing the waters" by placing an ad that would generate numerous resumes for future reference. In other cases the employer has a very broad salary range in mind but prefers looking at the salary history of candidates prior to committing a narrow salary range to the job. In many of these cases, the employer lets the market determine his or her salary range. We have noticed that far fewer ads mention a salary figure today than was the case even five years ago.

If you apply for a job which does not reveal a salary range, you will have to guess what salary is likely to be offered given your knowledge of jobs and salaries as well as your intuition. How do you make a "best guess" in such a situation? Obviously, you don't want to be too high nor too low. Neither do you want to waste time applying for jobs that are beneath your qualifications and experience. We suggest several approaches to dealing with this situation:

1. **Carefully analyze the listing for salary clues:** Look at each word and sentence for clues about the salary level of the position. Does the ad, for example, state minimum educational requirements? If the position requires a BA, it should be worth a minimum of $34,000 in most geographical areas. If the employer requires an MA, price the position at $40,000. Each year of required experience should be worth $2,000 for the first five years and $1,000 per year thereafter. Therefore, if the ad states minimum qualifications are a BA and three years of

progressive experience, price the job at $40,000. If the requirement is an MA and 10 years experience, price the job at $55,000. However, you may need to make some adjustments for regional variations. The baseline value of a BA and MA will differ from region to region. While they may be valued similarly in New York City, Boston, Washington, DC, San Francisco, and Los Angeles, they have different value in Albuquerque, Little Rock, and Peoria. Our shorthand method should bring you within 20 percent of the employer's salary range, which is close enough for finding common ground to negotiate. However, the figure will vary with the technical skills involved. A position requiring a liberal arts background may pay less while a position requiring hard-to-find technical skills will pay more.

If the position requires a BA, it should be worth at least $34,000. If the employer wants an MA, price the position at $40,000.

2. **Compare other ads that announce similar positions:** If you survey various publications and Internet sites with job listings, you should be able to find the same or similar positions with other companies that include salary ranges in the ads. After identifying five such ads, you will have a good idea of the going salary range for such a position.

3. **Contact individuals for salary information:** The quickest way to get salary information on the position is to call the personnel office of the company and frankly ask *"What is the salary range for this position?"* In many cases they will tell you. In other cases you won't know the name, address, or telephone number of the company, because you are responding to a blind ad. If this happens, call another company that might have a similar position and ask them if they know what might be the "going rate" for this type of position in the industry as a whole as well as in your region. You might also pose a similar question in a discussion group on the Internet (*"I'm applying for a position as a XXXX which requires XX years of experience. Do*

you know how much a position like this should pay in XXX city?") and hope you'll get accurate information.

Perhaps more important than guessing about the salary range for the position is **how** you respond to the ad. Most ads and application forms will request that you state in writing either your salary history or salary requirements. In fact, most employers are especially interested in your salary history because it gives them the most important information for valuing you as well as making you a salary offer which is likely to be no more than a 10- to 20-percent increase over your present or last salary. Whatever you do, beware of how you respond to these questions, because you may create a self-fulfilling prophecy which you will have to live with for many years – and many paychecks – to come.

Deal With Your Salary History

Regardless of how unfair it may seem, your last or present salary is the most powerful determiner of your next salary. To the surprise of many job seekers and employees, it really doesn't make much difference how important or productive you think you are, since employers are not particularly keen about paying new employees more than 15 percent above their past salary and current employees more than 5 percent above last year's salary. Therefore, employers want to know your salary history in order to determine your value. Once they have this information, they will extend a "reasonable" job offer. Individuals who do experience a major salary jump – a 30- to 100-percent increase – do so because their skills are especially in demand. Most employees seldom experience more than a 10-percent increase in salary.

How, then, do you deal with the question of salary history when you know full well that your answer is likely to become a self-fulfilling prophecy – your most recent salary plus 10 to 20 percent? Here you have several options, from being honest but dumb to lying to the employer.

The *"honest but dumb"* approach is to only state your net salary – your weekly or monthly take-home pay. While you may feel you are being completely honest, at the same time you can't get much dumber than this: you are revealing the very lowest amount of money you receive from a job! Welcome to the world of the salaried disadvantaged.

Respond Right to Ads and Applications

If you engage in lying, the sky is the limit on what you might tell the employer. Unfortunately, this lie may not take you very far, especially when the employer decides to check your earnings with your last employer or ask to see pay stubs for salary verification. While you may be clever enough to get your past employer to also lie as well as create some phony pay stubs, such deception is a high-risk approach. Some job applicants may use this approach successfully, but there is a high probability you will be "found out" and perhaps lose more than a chance at this job.

A third approach is to do some **creative, but truthful, calculating** when determining your salary history. At the very least you will want to start with your gross rather than your net pay. Then begin thinking in terms of **total compensation**, rather than just a base salary, which translates your benefits into a salary equivalent figure, as you did in Chapter 1 (pages 5-7) when you calculated your current and desired compensation. Indeed, given the flexible benefit packages now offered to many employees, some employees choose to receive many benefits as part of their salary. Since compensation packages are not necessarily equivalent among employers, make sure you are comparing apples with apples rather than apples with oranges. For example, wages may constitute only 60 or 70 percent of total compensation with some employers, but wages may constitute as much as 90 percent of compensation with other employers. A $50,000 a year salary figure with one employer may be equivalent to a $42,000 salary figure with other employers if certain benefits are not included in the compensation package.

Begin thinking in terms of total compensation rather than just a base salary which translates your benefits into a salary equivalent figure.

Most employers can put a dollar figure on benefits. Depending on what is included in your compensation package, you may want to multiply your gross monthly or yearly salary figure by 30 percent and add that additional amount to your base salary figure. For example, consider the case of an individual who makes $30,000 a year. The creative way to calculate salary that may also truthfully reflect the individual's total compensation is as follows:

Base yearly/ monthly salary	$30,000 a year ($2,500 per month at the beginning of the year but $3,000 per month at the end of the year)
Benefits	30% of base salary
Total compensation	$39,000

Another approach is to use your highest monthly salary, including any bonuses, as the baseline for calculating a new yearly salary figure. For example, if you made $30,000 last year for an average of $2,500 per month – but during the last two months you received a raise or additional compensation of $3,000 a month – use the $3,000 a month as your salary base. Therefore, your so-called $30,000 a year at $2,500 per month looks much lower than $30,000 a year but with a recent increase to $3,000 per month:

Yearly salary based on $3,000 per month	$36,000

In this case you should tell the employer that you make $3,000 per month or $36,000 a year. Better still, if you factor in an additional 30 percent for benefits, your total compensation picture will be:

Total compensation based on $3,000 per month salary	$46,800

Therefore, when you negotiate a salary which will likely be 15 to 20 percent above your present base, you will be talking about a salary close to $50,000. Had you not figured your salary history in this manner, you might be talking closer to $35,000.

A final approach to creatively calculating your salary history is to include additional work-related income in your total salary figure. If, for example, you do outside consulting work and you were lucky enough to make $500 to $1,000 a day on a project, factor this information into your salary figure. But don't be unrealistic by thinking you are worth $500 to $1,000 a day just because you happened to have one lucky day during the past year or two! Use this information as an indicator: you are potentially worth more than your normal salary. In addition, will this new job preclude you from engaging in outside income generating activities or will it allow you to either "daylight" or "moonlight"?

Educators are a special case in point when dealing with the question of salary history. Contrary to what many educators may think, they actually receive excellent salaries given the amount of time they really work. The major problem is that their yearly salary is only based upon seven to nine months of work. When figuring their salary history, educators should analyze their salary in terms of the hours, weeks, or months worked rather than a base yearly salary. If, for example, an educator makes $40,000 a year but in reality only works eight months out of the year, their salary is actually $5,000 per month or $60,000 a year. Indeed, many higher educators average $75,000 a year but only work eight or nine months out of the year. In addition, they have liberal opportunities to both "daylight" and "moonlight." Such a workload translates into the equivalent of $9,375 per month or $112,500 per year – not bad for what many people claim to be a poorly paid profession!

> *Individuals who only reveal monthly or yearly take-home pay literally commit salary suicide.*

While some employers may dispute the way you calculate salary history – since they, too, offer benefits that can be translated into salary equivalents – they eventually must face up to the fact that you are probably worth more than what your base salary indicates. Furthermore, they need to translate **their** benefit package into a salary equivalent amount for comparative purposes. The whole point of engaging in such creative salary calculations is to **stress your true value** which is higher than a base wage figure. Moreover, you should be financially rewarded on the basis of performance rather than on salary history. While you recognize that salary history is an important component in the employer's salary calculations, you are reluctant to accept a salary that is based on a 10 or 20-percent increase over your present salary.

If you initially deal with the salary history question in this manner, you will begin focusing the main thrust of your job search on how your performance will add value to the employer and the organization. This is exactly the point you want to consistently make from the initial application stage to the final job offer where you will negotiate the total compensation package in earnest.

Given these different ways of calculating so-called "salary history," it would be dumb to just reveal monthly or yearly take-home pay. Individuals that make this mistake literally commit salary suicide!

Now that you have several alternative ways of calculating your salary history, how should you respond to ads and applications that ask you to reveal your salary history? You have two major alternatives here:

1. **Leave this information off altogether in anticipation that you will deal with the question of salary when being interviewed for the job:** While it is always best to leave the salary question to the end – after you have demonstrated your value to the employee – this is not always possible. Many employers want to initially deal with the salary question in order to screen candidates in or out of the hiring process. If you don't provide this requested information, the employer may screen you out for having an incomplete application – you can't follow instructions! If you guess wrong and state too high or too low a salary figure, you may be screened out prematurely. This is one of those proverbial *"Damned if you do, damned if you don't"* situations. We have no best advice here except to examine other alternative ways of responding to the situation.

2. **State your salary history:** Make your best calculation based on knowledge of your total compensation as we indicated earlier. State either a monthly or yearly salary figure, whichever is highest. While this response will satisfy the employer's application requirement, it is risky in the sense that you may present too high or too low a figure in reference to the job. If it screens you out, so much the better. You don't want to waste your time with jobs that are above or beneath your qualifications, experience, and salary history. At least your response brings this application to an end so you can concentrate your efforts on other more appropriate jobs.

State Your Salary Requirements

Other ads and applications will ask you for your salary requirements. Your salary requirements are what you **expect to receive** regardless of what you have made in the past. These are your expectations.

Respond Right to Ads and Applications

You have a larger range of alternatives with this question than with salary history:

1. **Leave this information blank:** Rather than state an expected salary or salary range, don't respond to this question at all. The employer will assume you either forgot to include it or you are "open" to the employer's salary range.

2. **State "Open" or "Negotiable":** These terms indicate to the employer that you are flexible about salary and willing to negotiate. We prefer this approach to the salary expectation question, because it puts the question off. It gives you a chance to find out more about the position as well as communicate your qualifications to the interviewer. Everything you do between now and when you receive the job offer should be aimed at demonstrating your value to the employer. At the end you will want to translate your value into a specific salary range which will be negotiated into a specific salary figure. The more you can invest the employer's time in you, the better should be your negotiating position. You do this by keeping the salary question to the very last – after you have had a chance to both assess the position, employer, and organization and convince the employer that you are worth exactly what you expect to receive for this job.

    > *Everything you do should be aimed at demonstrating your value.*

3. **State a salary range:** If you have a good idea of the employer's salary range, indicate your salary range. However, make sure the bottom of your range overlaps with the top of the employer's range. For example, if the employer's range is $35,000 to $40,000, make your range $40,000 to $45,000. This gives you "common ground" around which to later negotiate a final salary figure.

Respond to Stated Salary Ranges

Many employment ads and vacancy announcements will state the salary or salary range for a position. However, the degree to which salary ranges are specified and the extent to which they are negotiable depends on the level and importance of the position. In general, the widest salary ranges are assigned to the most negotiable positions – high-level jobs. The lowest level jobs tend to have fixed salaries assigned to them, and few of these jobs are negotiable. What this means in practice is that if a position is valued under $25,000, the ad will normally state a specific figure, such as $21,250. If the position is valued between $25,000 and $50,000, the ad often includes a narrow salary range, such as $38,000 to $42,000. If the position is valued over $50,000, the range may be very broad or framed in the ultimate negotiable terms: $60,000+.

This salary range information gives important clues to how much flexibility you might have in negotiating.

A stated range gives you information on whether you want to consider the job as well as indicates that the employer has some flexibility in negotiating salary. How far above the top of the range he or she can negotiate is questionable, especially since many pay systems are relatively rigid. In general, however, employers have little flexibility to negotiate lower level salaries. They have greater flexibility to negotiate salaries for high-level positions. After all, top talent is a scarce commodity that must be acquired through flexible compensation policies that enable employers to negotiate what is necessary in order to acquire needed talent.

When you apply for a job that has a stated salary range, the employer assumes your salary history and expectations fit into his or her stated range. But your willingness to respond to the ad or vacancy announcement does not necessarily commit you to accepting the employer's salary range. This salary range information gives you important clues as to how much flexibility you might have in the final salary negotiation session. If you make the top of the employer's salary range the bottom of your salary range, you should have some room to negotiate. However, don't expect the employer to have much flexibility beyond the top of the stated salary range. Going beyond the top of the salary range only occurs when employers feel they are hiring an exceptionally qualified and promising candidate for the position.

Respond Right to Ads and Applications

In cases where employers cannot meet the salary expectations of their preferred candidate, nonetheless they may change their mind by going so far as to create a new position that would better accommodate the candidate's interests, skills, and abilities. Should you ever reach an impasse during salary negotiations, this "position transformation" approach is worth suggesting to an employer. You might ask if the company is willing to change the requirements of the position, or create a new position with a higher salary, for which you qualify?

If, on the other hand, you decide to apply for a job that is beneath or far above your salary history, be prepared to explain why you appear to be either over-qualified or under-qualified for the position. Such questions will eventually surface during the course of job interviews. Again, treat salary ranges as indications of the value of both the position and the employee who will occupy the position. If you are applying for a position that pays much higher than your salary history appears to justify, you will have to explain in detail how you acquired this sudden increase in value!

7

Communicate Your Value in Job Interviews

ONCE YOU'VE PASSED the initial application and screening stages of your job search, the next step is to be interviewed for a job. The interview can take many forms. It may start with a telephone call from the employer who is attempting to screen a pool of 10 possible candidates for identifying three finalists who will be invited to job interviews. If you become one of the finalists, you may actually go through two or three interviews – each being a different type – before being offered the job and arriving at a mutually satisfactory compensation agreement. At each interview, you should focus on communicating your **value** to the potential employer. How well you communicate that value will largely determine the shape of your compensation package. You must appear desirable – a star performer who will add to the bottom line.

Talking Salary at the Interview

During each stage of the job interview, the question of salary and compensation may arise unexpectedly. For example, as part of the telephone screening interview, the employer may ask you about your salary expectations or salary requirements. If not then, the employer may ask you the same question during the initial interview or during the second or third interview. Whatever the timing and scenario, you must be prepared to respond to the salary question at any time during your job search, for your answer to this one key question can quickly eliminate you from further consideration. A wrong answer can also result in under-valuing you for the position and being offered a salary lower than what you should receive had you been better prepared for the interview.

Interviewing Principles

As you prepare for any interview – be it a job interview or a meeting with your present employer to discuss your performance and future compensation – keep in mind several principles for asking and answering questions. These principles will help you focus on the most important goal of the interview – exchanging useful information for making a job decision.

While the major purpose of a resume is to communicate your qualifications to employers, the major purpose of the interview should be to communicate your **value** to employers. In the interview, your qualifications become translated into value which, in turn, is assigned a salary figure. How well you communicate your value in the interview will affect the size of your compensation package.

The major purpose of the interview should be to communicate your value to employers.

Many job hunters feel they need to practice answers to standard interview questions in order to impress interviewers. Indeed, many interview books, such as ***Best Answers to 202 Job Interview Questions*** and ***301 Smart Answers to Tough Interview Questions***, are filled with examples of questions and answers, which many readers assume they should practice as well as mimic during interviews. As a result, many job hunters learn to play the role of interviewee. They primarily give "canned" answers to interviewers' questions. After a while most interviewees sound the same as they give similar answers to interviewers' questions.

The problem with this approach is that it results in a form of role playing that communicates little content or value to employers. Your goal should be to communicate your **value** to employers rather than recite what many people consider to be correct answers to questions. You do this by following certain principles that help you formulate detailed answers as well as thoughtful questions which also communicate the "unique you" to employers.

You communicate your value to employers by the way in which you answer and ask questions. When answering and asking questions, you should try to engage in the following nine interview behaviors:

1. **When talking about yourself, be sure to focus on your major strengths and accomplishments as they relate to the employer's needs:** Throughout your job search, and especially during the interview, you should stress your most important qualities – your skills, strengths, and accomplishments. When employers put people on their payrolls, they are most interested in hiring specific skills that translate into productivity for the organization.

2. **Be sufficiently redundant on points that stress your benefits for the employer:** A certain level of redundancy is necessary in the interview. While you will cover many different subjects and issues relevant to the job during the interview, you should stress over and over again your major qualifications and your central value to the employer. Try to formulate answers that stress your **benefits** in reference to the position, employer, and organization. Employers are looking for benefits from their employees. The more you talk about benefits you will give the employer, the better you should do in the interview.

> Employers are looking for benefits from their employees.

3. **Turn potential negatives into positives:** While employers are looking for reasons to hire you, they are also looking for reasons not to hire you. Many interviewers ask questions designed to identify your weaknesses or negatives; they ask questions aimed at finding objections to hiring you. For example, the interviewer might ask you some negative questions about your background: *"What are your major weaknesses?"* or *"Why didn't you get better grades in school?"* or

Communicate Your Value in Job Interviews

"Why did you only stay in your first job for six months?" They may also raise objections to your salary requirements: *"How can I justify paying you this much when others in our organization, with similar qualifications and experience, are making less?"* or *"Why do you think you are worth that much, especially given the fact that you were making only $____ in your last job?"* Try to respond to these questions with positive answers that again stress your value. For example, your major weakness might be this:

> *I often get so involved with my work that I neglect my family. I'm learning to better balance my professional and personal lives.*

The reason you didn't get better grades in college might be the following:

> *I had hoped to do better, but I was carrying full course loads, working part-time, and participating 15 hours a week in student government.*

And one positive response to an objection to your salary requirements might be this:

> *I'm sure inequities exist in most organizations, and it's something employers want to eliminate in their efforts to be fair to all. I feel I should be compensated on the basis of my value and performance, as we've already discussed. Given what you've said about the role of the performance appraisal in determining compensation, I'm pleased that management is committed to rewarding employees according to their performance.*

4. **Be a good listener**: The more you can get the interviewer to talk about the position and organization, the better should be your position in the job interview. Listen carefully for clues about the value of the position and compensation policies of the organization. Answer the interviewer's questions in detail and by using positive form, but do be an attentive listener. You do

this by focusing your attention on the interviewer and what he or she is saying, overlooking irritating mannerisms and comments, withholding evaluations of messages received, and giving positive nonverbal feedback (nod in agreement, smile occasionally, make eye contact). Employers appreciate employees who are good listeners. Good listeners communicate a certain **attitude** that is welcomed by employers. And attitude is extremely important in a job interview. The right attitude communicates confidence.

5. **Become employer-centered rather than self-centered:** Focus on the needs of your audience rather than on your needs and wants. While you do want to talk about your accomplishments by using such active verbs as *"I completed," "I directed," "I supervised,"* or *"I initiated,"* you must also direct your attention to the employer's needs. Keep in mind that the employer has problems to solve. In fact, one reason you are being interviewed is that the employer needs to solve certain problems which you may be hired to resolve. The more you can talk in the language of the employer about solving his or her problems, the stronger will be your position in the interview process. Avoid talking about benefits you should receive from the employer until the very end when you negotiate the compensation package. If you talk about salary, vacation time, child care policies, stock options, and retirement plans early in the interview, you will communicate the wrong message to the employer – that you are looking for a place to reap benefits rather than generate additional value for the employer. You want to know what the employer can do for you rather than what you can do for the employer – an attitude that is not conducive to self-motivation and productivity. In other words, analyze your audience **before** addressing issues concerning your qualifications and value.

6. **Answer and ask questions directly and in detail:** An interviewer's questions deserve thoughtful, focused, and detailed answers. Avoid simple *"yes"* or *"no"* answers. Each question asked of you should become another opportunity for you to communicate your value to the employer. You cannot do this if

you prepare a set of stock role-playing answers to standard interview questions that others typically serve up to interviewers. Employers want to know how you can best solve their problems. You communicate your value by explaining exactly what you will do for the employer based on your previous experience and performance as well as your understanding of the position, employer, and organization.

7. **Use supports for making your points:** One of the best ways to express your value when providing detailed answers to questions is to use supports. These come in many forms: examples, illustrations, descriptions, definitions, statistics, comparisons, testimonials, or stories. If, for example, you want to communicate to the employer that you helped promote productivity on your last job, don't just state this accomplishment in general terms. Use an example that explains what you did or offer a statistic:

   By reorganizing the sales force into five new regional centers, I was able to increase sales by nearly 70 percent over the next 12-month period. This meant an additional $800,000 in profits and a much happier sales force.

8. **Give positive nonverbal clues and feedback:** Over 60 percent of what is communicated is done nonverbally. How you dress, sit, listen, smell, use eye contact, shake hands, and eat may be as or more important than how you respond verbally to questions. Be sure your nonverbal behaviors, especially your dress and appearance, are appropriate for the position. Dress and groom for the job you want, not for the one you have at present. For example, if you are interviewing for a position that pays $50,000 or more a year, dress like you are worth every penny of that salary – if not more. When asked about salary and the employer's salary range, make sure your nonverbal responses are consistent with your verbal response. Don't nod your head in agreement while you are saying you were thinking of a higher salary. Such nonverbal behavior contradicts your verbal behavior and thus may raise questions about your honesty in dealing with the employer.

9. Help the interviewer through the process: Contrary to what many interviewees may think, not all interviewers are experts in conducting job interviews and negotiating salaries. For many, the interview is an intrusion into their important day-to-day job routines. Not surprisingly, many interviewers do not ask the most important questions or they fail to follow-through on others. The more you can help the interviewer get through this process, the better should be your position with the interviewer. If, for example, the interviewer forgets to ask about your major achievements, you might volunteer this question in the form of an observation relevant to the position by mentioning that your experience seems to have prepared you well for this position. You should then detail your relevant accomplishments as they relate to the position. Keep with you a written list of pertinent points you want to make regarding your qualifications as well as questions you need to ask the interviewer. In fact, the questions you ask the interviewer may be more important than the answers you give to the interviewer's questions. If you fail to remember all of them, near the end of the interview you should mention to the interviewer that you have a few questions you wanted to ask. Then refer to your list as you ask questions you need answered, or take this opportunity to stress your accomplishments so you can best communicate your value.

Initiating the Salary Question

Who should initiate the question of compensation? As any negotiating expert will tell you, it's always preferable to have the other person expose his or her hand first so you will have some idea of that person's negotiating parameters and the base or ranges from which you are operating in reference to him/her. The old bargaining adage *"He who reveals his hand first is likely to lose the most"* is especially relevant when negotiating salary. Ideally, you want the employer to reveal early on in the interview something to this effect: *"For your information, the salary range for this position is $40,000 to $45,000."*

Few employers are up-front about their specific salary figures during the interview. Instead, they want you to expose your hand first by asking you one of two questions, or both: *"What are your salary expectations for this position? What are you making at present?"* Somewhere during the interviews, both of you will have to answer each other's question. But who goes first may be critical to the final salary outcome.

The major principle you should follow for addressing the salary question is to try to **neutralize** it until the very last interview, which should be the interview where you are extended a job offer contingent upon reaching a satisfactory compensation agreement. The reason you want to do this is very simple: the two-fold purpose of your job search, especially the job interview, has been to communicate your qualifications to employers and determine whether the job is right for you. When addressing the issue of compensation, qualifications mean your value as translated into salary and benefits. If you prematurely address the compensation question by discussing dollars and cents prior to communicating your value to the employer, you will commit a serious error in judgment: both you and the employer have decided on price **before** looking at the product. Chances are you will decide on a low price since few employers are about to pay a high price at this stage of the hiring process.

> **Neutralize the salary questions until the very last interview.**

But there are practical limitations to what extent you will be successful in neutralizing the compensation issue. After all, employers have an interest in learning as soon as possible about your salary history and salary requirements. Therefore, you must be prepared to answer the employer's questions about compensation early in the interview. The best way to neutralize such questions is to respond, with some variation, in the following manner:

> *If you don't mind, I would prefer giving you a specific answer after I've had a chance to learn more about the position and your organization. I'm sure we can reach mutual agreement at that time.*

While this is a good response for neutralizing the employer's question, you should also take the employer's question as an opportunity to learn more about the position, the organization, and the employer. In other words, you want to do more than just neutralize this question by pushing it off until the very last interview. Indeed, this is a good time for you to initiate an important line of questioning about the value of the position and the internal personnel policies of the organization. For example, you might ask several of these questions:

- What are the duties and responsibilities assigned to this position?

- Does this position involve extensive travel and overtime?

- Whom would I be working with, and how many people might I be supervising?

- Would I have my own budget?

- How much money would I be responsible for handling in this position?

- Whom would I report to?

- How does your organization structure its pay system, personnel policies, and promotions as well as dispense rewards?

- Is performance important for compensation increases and promotions, or is seniority a key factor?

- How does the performance appraisal operate in terms of rewarding individual and group performance?

- What are some of the problems the previous individuals in this job experienced in terms of responsibilities, people, and performance?

- What three things do most employees really like about working here? (If compensation is not at the top three, take note and follow through with another question – *"On a scale of 1 to 10, how do you think your employees would rate your company in terms of compensation?"*)

By responding to the compensation question in this manner, you indicate to the employer that you have important questions that go to the heart of the position and organization. You need to know more about the position, employer, and organization before you can seriously talk about money. Employers understand the importance of these questions and will respect you for such a response. Above all, you indicate that you are a serious candidate who needs to learn more about the position and organization before making an employment decision. A response that moves the discussion to key compensation issues is much more impressive to employers than just delaying the discussion of salary until the very end of the interview where you may be perceived as someone who is playing the silent game of hard-to-get.

Answering the Salary Question

Delaying the salary question to the very end is not always possible nor practical given the demands placed on you by some interviewers. When the salary question arises – assuming you cannot or do not want to put it off until later – you should do one of two things. First, you can turn the question around by asking *"What is the salary range for this position?"* or *"How much is budgeted?"* or *"How much would someone with my qualifications and experience receive in this position?"*

Delaying the salary question to the very end is not always possible.

A second response is more forthcoming and directly addresses the salary issue. Your first step should be to clearly **summarize** the job duties and responsibilities as you understand them. At this point you are attempting to do two things:

- Seek clarification from the interviewer as to the actual job and all it involves.

- Emphasize the level of skills required in the most positive way. In other words, you emphasize the value and worth of this position to the organization, and subtly this may help support the actual salary figure that the interviewer or you later provide.

You might do this, for example, by saying,

> *As I understand it, I would report directly to the vice president in charge of marketing, and I would have full authority for marketing decisions that involved expenditures of up to $100,000. I would have a staff of five people – a secretary, two copywriters, and two marketing assistants.*

Such a summary statement establishes for you and the interviewer that this position (1) reports to the highest levels of authority; (2) is responsible for decision-making involving fairly large sums of money; and (3) involves supervision of staff.

Although you may not explicitly draw the connection, you are emphasizing the value of this position to the organization. This position should be worth a lot more than one in which the hiree will report to the marketing manager, be required to get approval for all expenditures over $100, and has no staff – just access to the secretarial pool! By doing this, you will focus the salary questions (that you have not yet responded to) around the exact work you must perform on the job in exchange for salary and benefits. You have also seized the opportunity to focus on the value of the person who will be selected to fill this vacancy.

Your conversation might go something like this. The employer poses the question:

What are your salary requirements?

Your first response should be to summarize the responsibilities of the position:

> *Let me see if I understand all that is involved with this position and job. I would be expected to _____ _____. Have I covered everything or are there some other responsibilities I should know about?*

This response focuses the salary question around the value of the position in relation to you. After the interviewer responds to your final question, answer the initial salary expectation question in this manner:

What is the normal range in your company for a position such as this?

This question establishes the value as well as the range for the **position or job** – two important pieces of information you need before proceeding further into the salary negotiation stage. The employer normally will give you the requested salary range. Once he or she does, depending on how you feel about the figure, you can follow up with one more question:

What would be the normal salary range for someone with my qualifications?

This question further establishes the value for the **individual** versus the position. This line of questioning will yield the employer's salary expectations without revealing your desired salary figure or range. It also indicates whether the employer distinguishes between individuals and positions when establishing salary figures.

At this stage you are prepared to state your expected salary. You can either state a specific figure or a salary range. As we will see in the next chapter, when we examine the negotiation process, it's preferable to state a range. Your best strategy is to place the top of the employer's range at the bottom of your range. This gives you common ground from which to negotiate the final offer. If you do this, you should be able to increase your salary above the employer's norm.

Questions You Need to Answer

During the job interview you will be asked numerous questions about your education, work experience, career goals, and personality. If you have been invited to an interview, the employer has already decided that you have the necessary skills to perform the job. What employers are most interested in is meeting you in person to determine if you will "fit in" with their organization. They want to know what kind of person you are. What about your attitudes, motivations, and goals in relation to work, employers, and your future? Are you the type of person who is likely to get along well with others in the organization? How do you dress and interact socially with others? Employers also want to settle the question of compensation if they decide to offer you the job. While they prefer that you accept what they initially offer you, most employers also expect to negotiate salary and benefits – especially for high-level positions.

You can expect the interviewer will ask you many of these questions in the process of determining your value:

Education

- Describe your educational background.
- Why did you attend _____ University (or College)?
- Why did you major in _____?
- What was your grade point average?
- What subjects did you enjoy the most? The least? Why?
- What leadership positions did you hold?
- How did you finance your education?
- If you started all over, what would you change about your education?
- Why were your grades so low? So high?
- Did you do the best you could in school? If not, why not?

Work Experience

- Why did you change jobs before?
- What do you most enjoy doing?
- What were your major achievements in each of your past jobs?
- What did you like about your boss? Dislike?
- Which job did you enjoy the most? Why?
- Which job did you enjoy the least? Why?
- Have you ever been fired? Why?
- What skills will you bring to this job?

Career Goals

- What ideally would you like to do?
- Why are you looking for another job?
- Why should we hire you?
- What do you want to be doing five years from now?
- What are your short-range and long-range career goals?
- What other types of jobs are you considering? Companies?

Communicate Your Value in Job Interviews

Personal Considerations

- Tell me about yourself.
- What are you major weaknesses? Your major strengths?
- What causes you to lose your temper?
- What do you do in your spare time? Do you have any hobbies?
- What types of books do you read?
- What role does your family play in your career?
- How well do you work under pressure? In meeting deadlines?
- Tell me about your management philosophy.
- What kind of work environment do you prefer?
- What really motivates you to be productive?
- On a scale of 1 to 10, how much initiative do you normally take?
- What types of people do you prefer working with?
- How _____ (creative, analytical, tactful, etc.) are you?
- If you could change your life, what would you do differently?
- Who are your references?
- How much do you use the Internet?
- Do you consider yourself Internet savvy?
- What are some of your favorite websites?

Judgment

- Why do you want to join our organization?
- Why do you think you are qualified for this position?
- How would you improve our operations?
- What attracted you to our company?
- If you could choose your job and organization, where would you go?

Compensation

- What are you making at present?
- How much were you making on your last job?
- What are your salary requirements?
- What is the lowest pay you will take?

- How much do you think you are worth for this job?
- How much do you want to be making in five years?
- Why should we pay you more than others in our organization who have similar qualifications and experience?

While these are standard interview questions most employers ask, more and more employers also are asking behavior-based questions these days. For example, you might be asked *"Can you tell me how you improved your employer's just-in-time inventory system during the past six months?"* Such a question attempts to identify patterns of behavior that may or may not be suitable for the job under consideration. Responding well to such performance questions requires story-telling skills which include examples of your specific accomplishments. Indeed, you should be responding with examples and quantification of your accomplishments throughout your interview in order to demonstrate your value to the employer. If you do well with behavior-based questions, you should be in a strong position to negotiate a salary that clearly reflects your value.

Anticipate these as well as other questions the interviewer might ask so you can prepare well thought-out responses prior to the interview. It is far easier to formulate positive responses to interview questions in the relaxed setting of your study than in the stressful and time-constrained setting of the job interview.

Questions You Should Ask

As you prepare for the interview, you also should outline questions you want to ask the prospective employer. You need to ask questions to elicit information **you** need about the position and organization; indeed, you want to know if the position is fit for you. In addition, your interests, qualifications, personality, and competence will be partly judged by the number and types of questions you ask the interviewer. By the very act of asking intelligent questions, you give yourself additional value in the eyes of employers.

What types of questions should you ask in order to get information about the job as well as impress the interviewer about your value? In general, questions relating to job duties, responsibilities, opportunities for training, and employee advancement within the company are appropriate.

Communicate Your Value in Job Interviews

Avoid asking self-centered questions during initial interviews or early stages of the interview unless they are raised first by the interviewer. Of course you are interested in salary, but you do not want to create the impression it is your primary concern. Remember, your prospective employer is interested in what **benefits** you will bring to the organization. At the same time, you need to **establish your value** in the eyes of the employer prior to discussing money.

The following set of questions outline some of the most common questions interviewees should ask:

- What duties and responsibilities does this job entail?
- Where does this position fit into the organization?
- Is this a new position?
- What kind of person are you looking for?
- When was the last person promoted?
- What is the best experience and background for this position?
- Whom would I report to? Tell me a little about these people. Are you happy with them? What are their strengths and weaknesses?
- What are your expectations for me?
- May I talk with present and previous employees about this job and organization?
- What problems might I expect to encounter on this job? (efficiency, quality control, declining profits, internal politics)
- What has been done recently in regards to _____?
- What is the normal pay range for this job?
- How are raises and promotions determined?
- How do you measure and reward performance?
- On a scale of 1 to 10, how would most employees rate this company? What do they like the most about working here? How do they feel about compensation?
- How did you get your job?
- How long have you been with this company?
- Tell me about promotions and advancement here.
- What might I expect for myself?
- What does the future look like for this company?

By formulating questions prior to the interview, you demonstrate concern about the position as well as preparation for the interview. Interviewers should view you in a positive manner for doing this.

Use Positive Form

The way you phrase your questions and answers can be as important as the actual content of your communication when conveying your value to employers. What you want to achieve is **positive form**. This means avoiding negatives by presenting yourself in as positive a light as possible. In the interview, several opportunities arise for enhancing your image through the use of positive form.

The first use of positive form relates to **names**. Each of us likes to be called by an appropriate name. Make sure you get the name of the interviewer, get it right, and use it from time to time as you speak. Use the interviewer's title (Miss, Mrs., Mr., Dr., Professor, etc.) and last name. **Never** call the interviewer by his or her first name unless specifically requested to do so – even if the interviewer uses your first name. Many interviewers will be offended by such familiarity.

A second use of positive form is inherent in the **way you phrase questions and answers**. For example, rather than ask *"What are the duties of _____ position?,"* ask *"What would be my duties?"* This form of questioning subtly plants the positive thought of you in the position. This is not presumptuous because you use the word *"would,"* which indicates you are not overly sure of yourself.

A third use of positive form relates to **good grammar**. Proper use of language is not something to be left in the English classroom. Many so-called "educated" people do not use good grammar, and many of these people do not interview successfully. By all means, check your use of grammar. If it is not impeccable, make an effort to improve it before the interview.

Fourth, use **good diction**. One of the most common problems is to shorten words. How many people do you hear say *"goin"* instead of *"going,"* or *"gonna"* rather then *"going to"*? Another problem is substituting, eliminating, or adding consonants: *"Adlanta"* rather than *"Atlanta," "din't"* rather than *"didn't," "idear"* rather than *"idea."* Do you do this? Do you ever say *"yea"* rather *"yes"*? The use of sloppy speech is a habit many people, including the well educated, get into. But it is a habit – a learned and reinforced behavior – you can change. If you have a tendency to modify words like this, it is a habit worth correcting.

Fifth, avoid using **vocalized pauses**. An occasional silence is acceptable and preferable to overuse of *"ah"* and *"uhm."* Try not to fill silences with *"ah"* or *"and ah."* Vocalized pauses distract the listener from your message, and the excessive use can be annoying as well as lessen your credibility.

Sixth, avoid the use of **fillers**. Fillers add no information and, if overdone, also distract the listener. The most commonly used fillers are *"you know,"* *"like"* and *"okay."* If they are used frequently, the listener becomes distracted and will find it hard to concentrate on the content of your message.

Seventh, use **active verbs**. When talking about what you have done or will do, active verbs like *"organized,"* *"analyzed,"* or *"supervised"* are preferable to the nouns *"organizer,"* *"analyst,"* or *"supervisor."* Even stronger action words can be used to indicate your present strengths: *"organize,"* *"analyze,"* and *"supervise."* Avoid the passive voice. For example, instead of saying *"The entire conference was organized by me"* (passive), say *"I organized the entire conference"* (active).

Eighth, avoid using **tentative, indecisive terms**, such as *"I think,"* *"I guess,"* *"I feel."* If you use them excessively, they will negatively affect the impression you are trying to leave with the interviewer. Research indicates that women use these tentative terms more frequently than men. By using these indecisive terms, you can – male or female – appear indecisive and somewhat muddled. You want to communicate that you are a clear and purposeful individual.

Ninth, avoid the use of ambiguous and somewhat **negative terms** such as *"pretty good"* or *"fairly well."* These terms say little if anything. They may even communicate negatives – that what you did was not good!

Most people could improve their use of positive form. But it is difficult for someone to follow those suggestions after reading them the night before the interview. One needs to begin making the necessary changes well in advance of the interview. It can be done if one really wants to make the changes, but for most people it takes concerted effort over time. By all means, do not pass up the nine opportunities for using positive form in the interview.

Analyze Your Listener

Public speakers are always advised to analyze both their audience and their situation before speaking. The same advice should be followed when you interview. **The language you use should vary according to the interviewer.** If the interviewer is from the personnel office with little or no background in your field of expertise, your language should be less technical than it would be if you were talking with someone who shares your technical background. If you are interviewing with someone in your area of expertise, who also has the technical background, you should use a vocabulary relevant to the job in order to build common ground as well as your credibility. But don't overdo the use of jargon.

> *Present your strengths–major skills and accomplishments– in a positive way.*

Analysis of your situation should tell you this is not the time for excessive modesty. Of course, you do not want to become an obnoxious braggart, but you do want to present your strengths – skills and accomplishments – in a positive way. Therefore, don't be reluctant to **talk about yourself and your accomplishments**. Remember, the interviewer wants to know more about you, especially your potential value to him or her. The more positive information you can communicate to the interviewer, the stronger your position will be in the final hiring decision.

A frequent question asked by prospective interviewees is *"How honest should I be?"* Most individuals have something in their background they believe would work against them in getting the job if the interviewer knew about it. They wonder if they should tell the interviewer before he or she finds out. We advise you to be honest – but not stupid. In other words, if asked a direct question about the thing you hoped to hide, answer honestly, but emphasize positives. Under no circumstances should you volunteer your negatives or weaknesses.

Manage Questions With Positive Content

The actual content of your answers should be stated in the positive. One example of this is the type of hobbies you communicate to employers. As John Molloy notes, many employers prefer "active" hobbies, such as swimming, tennis, golfing, or jogging, to more sedentary activities, such as reading or stamp collecting.

But the most important examples of positive content relate to managing the specific interview questions which are designed to probe your knowledge, abilities, motivations, strengths, and weaknesses. The employer's goal is somewhat negative in the interview; he or she wants to know why **not** to hire you. The major unstated question is *"What are your weaknesses?"* Several other questions may be asked to indirectly answer this major one.

You should always phrase your answers to questions in a positive manner that stresses your value. Avoid the use of such commonly used negatives as *"can't," "didn't,"* and *"wouldn't."* These terms direct listeners into negative avenues of thinking. They do not communicate optimism and enthusiasm – two qualities you should demonstrate in the interview. Take, for example, two different answers to the following interview question:

QUESTION: Why did you major in business administration?

ANSWER 1: That's real funny. I wanted to major in history, but my parents told me if they were footing the bills, I shouldn't be studying useless subjects. I tried political science, biology, and accounting but didn't like any of them. Business administration wasn't that difficult for me. I couldn't think of anything I like more – except perhaps history. And it's not a bad field to be in these days.

ANSWER 2: I always enjoyed business and wanted to make it a career. As a youth I had my own paper route, sold books door to door, and was a member of Junior Achievement. In college I was involved in a couple of small businesses. It seems as though I have always been in business. I tend to have a knack for it, and I love it. My major in business administration further strengthened my desire to go into business. It gave me better direction. What I want is to work with a small and growing firm that would use my abilities to plan and implement marketing strategies.

While the first answer is truthful, it presents a negative and haphazard image of you. The second answer is also truthful, but it stresses the positive by communicating strengths, purpose, and enthusiasm.

Let's take as another example an employer who asks the interviewee why he is leaving his present job:

QUESTION: **Why are you leaving your present job?**

ANSWER 1: After working there three years, I don't feel I'm going anywhere. Morale isn't very good, and the management doesn't reward us according to our productivity. I really don't like working there anymore.

ANSWER 2: After working there three years, I have learned a great deal about managing people and developing new markets. But it is time for me to move on to a larger and more progressive organization where I can use my marketing experience in several different areas. I am ready to take on more responsibilities. This change will be a positive step in my professional growth.

> *Your language should project your strengths, purpose, and enthusiasm.*

Again, the first answer communicates too many negatives. The second answer is positive and upbeat in its orientation toward skills, accomplishments, and the future.

Most interview questions can be answered by using positive language that further emphasizes that you are competent, intelligent, friendly, spontaneous, honest, and likable. This language should project your strengths, purpose, and enthusiasm. If you feel you need to practice formulating positive responses to interview questions, examine the sample questions outlined earlier in this chapter. Consider alternative positive responses to each question. You also may want your spouse or friend to ask you interview questions. Tape record the "interview" and review your responses. Are your answers positive in both form and content? Do they communicate your strengths, purpose, and enthusiasm? Keep practicing the "interview" until you automatically respond with positive yet truthful answers.

Overcome Objections and Negatives

Interviewers are likely to have certain objections to hiring you. Some of their objections may be legitimate whereas others are misunderstandings. Among these objections are questions relating to your bona fide qualifications – education, experience, and skills.

If you are weak in any of the qualification areas, you may not be able to overcome the objections unless you acquire the necessary qualifications. But chances are these qualifications have been screened prior to the interview and thus will not be a topic of discussion. If, on the other hand, your education, experience, and skill level pose any objections in the mind of the interviewer, stress again your strengths in a positive and enthusiastic manner. Objections to your educational background will be the easiest to deal with if your experience and skills demonstrate your value.

On the other hand, one objection individuals increasingly encounter today from employers is being **over-qualified**. More and more people by choice are moving **down** in their careers rather than up. Given the desire for and ease of higher education, more and more people appear over-educated for many jobs today.

Employers' objections to candidates being over-qualified are a legitimate concern. From the perspective of employers, the over-qualified individual may quickly become a liability. Becoming unhappy with the job, they may leave after a short period of time. Other individuals may have an unrealistic ambition of quickly moving up the organizational ladder. In either case, the over-qualified individual may cost an employer more than he or she is worth.

On the other hand, the over-qualified candidate may think he or she is doing the employer a favor – the company is getting more for their money. If this is your perception of your value, you need to change it immediately. Unless you are prepared to take a position which is beneath your qualifications and can clearly communicate your desire to the employer so as to lessen his or her fears, you will most likely not get the job. In the interview you must convince the employer that you understand his or her apprehension about you, but you are willing, able, and eager to do the job.

While you want to communicate your strengths, employers want to know your weaknesses. There are several ways to handle questions that try to get at your weaknesses. If the interviewer frankly asks you *"What are some of your weaknesses?,"* be prepared to give him or her positive responses. You can do this in any of four different ways:

1. Discuss a negative which is not related to the job being considered:

> I don't enjoy accounting. I know it's important, but I find it boring. Even at home my wife takes care of our books. I really enjoy marketing. Other people are much better at bookkeeping than I am. I'm glad this job doesn't involve any accounting!

2. Discuss a negative which the interviewer already knows:

> I spent a great deal of time working on advanced degrees, as indicated on my resume, and thus I lack extensive work experience. However, I believe my education has prepared me well for this job. My leadership experience in college taught me how to work with people, organize, and solve problems. I write well and quickly. My research experience helped me analyze, synthesize, and develop strategies.

3. Discuss a negative which you managed to improve upon:

> I used to get over-committed and miss important deadlines. But then I read a book on time management and learned what I was doing wrong. Within three weeks I reorganized my use of time and found I could meet my deadlines with little difficulty. The quality of my work also improved. Now I have time to work out at the gym each day. I'm doing more and feeling better at the same time.

4. Discuss a negative that can also be a positive:

> I'm somewhat of a workaholic. I love my work, but I sometimes neglect my family because of it. I've been going into the office seven days a week and often work 12-hour days. I'm learning to better manage my time.

Take Initiative

Employment recruiters indicate that the most appealing candidates are those who take some initiative during the interview. We are not suggesting that you take control of the interview, but you need not play a completely passive role either. Taking initiative is a quality many employers prize in their employees. Indeed, many employers wish they could find more employees who would take initiative!

Even with the best interviewer, you will need to ask questions. Remember, you have a decision to make too. You need answers to some important questions about your future. Be sure you consider these questions:

- Are you really interested in the job?

- Does it fit your goals and skills?

- Will it give you the chance to do something you do well and enjoy doing?

- Will it give you an opportunity to move in some of the directions you want to move?

- What is the long-term value of this position in terms of developing your skills, experience, and professional networks?

Address these questions **before** you value the position and discuss compensation. A challenging job that enables you to acquire new skills and build important networks for career advancement is worth a lot more in terms of personal satisfaction and future professional growth than one that may offer an initial high salary. Always keep in mind the long-term value of a job.

Use the interview situation to get answers to these and other questions that are critical to your future. When you get to the final set of questions concerning compensation, you should be well prepared to negotiate a salary based upon knowledge of the value of both you and the position. You will put your best foot forward by stressing your strengths and by formulating answers and posing questions with positive form. You will approach the salary issue as a well qualified, positive, and enthusiastic future employee.

8

Negotiate the Best Compensation Package

WHILE THE SALARY question can arise anytime during a job interview, it is the central issue when you receive a job offer. In fact, you should never accept a job offer until you have solved the issue of compensation. Put another way, the employer may say *"We are prepared to offer you the job as long as we can reach agreement on compensation."* At this point the nature of the interview shifts toward benefits **you** will receive from the organization in exchange for **your** talents. No longer must you be only employer-centered. It's time to be somewhat self-centered as you translate your value and the value of the position into dollars, cents, and value equivalent benefits.

Go For It!

This is not the time to be shy about money. You must address the compensation question head-on in as professional but earnest a manner as possible. For the salary figure you agree on at this time will largely set the stage for future salary increments which are likely to be figured as a percentage of your base salary. Your basic goal should be to negotiate the highest salary possible as an indication that you will offer excellent value to the employer and the organization. How you arrive at a mutually agreeable figure requires strong negotiation skills.

Levels of Flexibility

Contrary to what some negotiation experts may tell you, not everything is negotiable. When it comes to salary and benefits, most employers have little flexibility to negotiate beyond very narrow ranges assigned to positions. Part of the reason is that most organizations have relatively rigid pay systems that are designed to be equitable and easy to administer. In many cases this rigidity is backed by laws designed to minimize discrimination based upon race, sex, and age. In part it is due to the fact that most positions are low to medium-level positions – the ones with the least salary flexibility.

> *Contrary to what negotiation experts may tell you, not everything is negotiable.*

When we say not everything is negotiable, we primarily refer to levels of flexibility among various positions within organizations. Expect to find three levels of salary flexibility in most organizations based upon the level of the position within the organizational hierarchy. The general principle for negotiating salaries is this: higher level positions are the most negotiable; lower level positions are the least negotiable. Three levels of negotiations apply to different salary ranges:

1. **Positions paying less than $30,000 a year:** Most of these positions are assigned a specific hourly or yearly salary figure. At this level employers need not negotiate salaries for several reasons: these are the most numerous positions with easily identified salary comparables found in the organization; many are entry-level positions; laws govern salary discrimination at this level; unions negotiate group contracts for many workers at this level; and an over-supply of candidates are available to fill these positions. As a result, the salary structure for these positions is the most rigid of any within most organizations. What flexibility exists may involve only a few

hundred dollars of negotiating room – a form of token negotiation – or a flexible benefits package which is equitably administered throughout the organization.

2. **Positions paying between $30,000 and $75,000 a year:** These mid-level positions may only constitute 20 percent of the total workforce within an organization. Most will be technical and professional positions which normally are assigned narrow salary ranges, depending on an individual's qualifications and experience. While employers have more flexibility to negotiate salaries in these pay ranges, pay systems still limit their degree of flexibility. Consequently, don't expect employers to be able to negotiate more than 15 percent above their stated salary figure. The stated range for many of these positions is between 10 and 20 percent. For example, a job paying $40,000 a year may have a salary range between $37,000 and $43,000. A $60,000 a year job may be assigned a range between $55,000 and $65,000. If you hope to go beyond a position's narrow salary range, you may need to focus your attention on redefining the position or creating a new position that has a higher salary range.

3. **Positions paying more than $75,000 a year:** Employers usually have the most flexibility in negotiating salaries in the $75,000+ range. These are normally top-level management positions which require special skills and experience that are hard to find in the marketplace. In addition, recruiting for these positions may be quite different than recruiting for the mid- and low-level positions. Employers, for example, may contract-out the hiring to specialized executive recruitment firms. Candidates, in turn, may use intermediaries to negotiate their compensation packages. It would not be unusual for someone offered a salary of $150,000 a year to negotiate a compensation package worth twice this figure. This big-bucks negotiating involves much more flexibility on the part of the employer who places much higher value on these positions than other positions in the organization. Since

many of these positions are not part of the rigid pay system, they are "open" and fully "negotiable" when it comes to questions of salary and benefits.

Whatever you do, avoid approaching employers with the idea that salaries for all positions are negotiable. The principles of salary negotiation are disproportionately distributed to the fewest number of positions. Some salaries are negotiable, but many aren't. And many that are negotiable are only negotiable within very limited ranges. The degree to which a position is negotiable depends on the position, the employer, the organization, and your perceived value. In other words, many positions are more or less negotiable depending on several factors. You will have some idea to what degree a position is negotiable once you discuss compensation, including the company's pay system, with the employer. This should occur prior to or during the salary negotiation session.

Negotiating Techniques

Once you reach the negotiating stage and have some idea of the employer's degree of salary flexibility, you should be prepared to negotiate the highest salary possible. Here you have several negotiating techniques from which to choose. Most of these techniques are appropriate for positions in the $30,000 to $75,000 a year range as well as for individuals who negotiate their own salaries above $75,000 a year. If you use a salary negotiating intermediary, such as a professional headhunter or employment agency representative who has strong salary negotiating skills, you need not get involved in this negotiating scenario.

After identifying what salary the employer is likely to offer, as discussed in Chapter 7, you have several choices on how to best approach the salary question. During the salary negotiation interview the employer will either ask you, *"What are your salary requirements?,"* or identify what he or she is prepared to offer: *"We are prepared to offer you a salary of $45,000 a year. Would that be satisfactory?"* Each question should elicit a different response from you. In the case of the first question, you should not be the one to volunteer a salary figure. It is to your advantage to have the employer reveal what he or she is prepared to offer you. If you state your salary requirement first, you might give too high or too low a figure and thus cede the salary advantage to the employer. If and when this question arises, try turning it around so the employer reveals the salary range earmarked for the position:

EMPLOYER: **What are your salary requirements?**

YOU: *If I remember correctly, this is the first time we've talked about the salary for this position. Could you tell me what the salary range is for this position as well as for someone with my qualifications?*

Unless the employer is playing a game with you, he or she should reveal the salary which is the amount budgeted for the position. Pause for a few seconds as you indicate nonverbally that you are thinking it over. By all means avoid looking overly enthusiastic or terribly disappointed. Remember, this is the time to negotiate a salary that should be either at the top of the employer's budgeted range, or beyond. In fact, silence is often golden at this stage of the salary negotiation session. If you remain silent for a least 30 seconds, the employer may begin to feel uneasy about the offer and actually increase it without you saying a word! The response to your silence might be, *"I think we can go $48,000. How would that be?"*

Silence is often golden. Your silence in response to an offer may immediately result in a higher offer!

Once you know the employer's salary range, you should be prepared to do some hard but professional bargaining. At this point you can respond to the employer's salary range four different ways. First, you can indicate that the employer's figure is acceptable to you and thus conclude your final interview. Second, you can haggle for more money in the hope of reaching an acceptable compromise. Third, you can delay final action by asking for more time to consider the figure. Finally, you can tell the employer the figure is unacceptable and leave.

The first and the last options indicate you are either too eager or you are playing hard-to-get. We recommend the second and third options. If you decide to reach agreement on salary in this interview, haggle in a professional manner. You can do this best by establishing a **salary range** from which to bargain in relation to the employer's salary range. For example, if the employer indicates that he or she is prepared to offer $40,000 to $45,000, and these figures are consistent with the salary data you gathered from your research, you should immediately **establish common ground** for negotiation. You do this by stating your own salary range which overlaps the employer's range. Pause for a few seconds as you think about this offer. In fact, a 30-second phase could result in a higher job offer! Then slowly respond. For example, if the employer's range is $40,000 to $45,000, respond by saying:

Yes, that does come near what I was expecting. I'm thinking in terms of $45,000 to $50,000.

You, in effect, **place the top of the employer's range into the bottom of your range**. By doing this you spread the range an additional $5,000 and put yourself into the high end. At this point you may be able to negotiate a final salary of $43,000 or $48,000, depending on how much flexibility the employer has with salaries or how willing he or she is in going to bat for you to justify a salary above the budgeted range. At the very least, assuming you supported your qualifications, you have made it more likely that the employer will agree to $45,000 rather than try to get you for $40,000.

> *Most employers have more flexibility with salary ranges than they are willing to admit.*

Most employers have more flexibility with salary ranges than they are willing to admit. They will find the money to hire you if they are convinced they are hiring top talent. Indeed, it would be foolish for them not to consider the fact that you will probably give them a much better return for their money than other candidates, especially when only a few hundred or thousand dollars separate you from a final agreement. And since the employer has already invested much time in you, unless there is a strong second candidate, it will probably cost the organization more than $1,500 to recruit someone else for this position.

Once you have placed your expectations at the top of the employer's salary range, you need to again emphasize your value. Remember the **supports** we discussed in previous chapters. It is not enough to simply state you were "thinking" in a certain range; you must state **why** you believe you are worth what you want. Ideally, your explanation should be based on facts, centered around the employer's interests, and stress the benefits you will bring to the organization. You might say, for example,

> *The salary surveys I've read indicate that the salary for the position of _____ in this industry and region is between $45,000 and $50,000. Since, as we have discussed, I have extensive experience in all the areas you outlined, I would not need training in the job duties themselves – just a brief orientation to the operating procedures you use here at ____. I'm sure I could be up and running in this job within a week or two. Taking everything in consideration – especially my skills and experience and what I see as my future contributions to your company – I really feel a salary of $50,000 is fair compensation. Is this possible here at _____?*

Always keep in mind that you should negotiate from a position of strength, not need or greed. To be most effective in negotiating a salary that reflects your true value, you need to establish your value; learn what the employer is willing to pay; keep your salary rationale employer-centered in stressing benefits; and negotiate in a professional manner. How you handle the salary negotiation will affect your future relations with the employer. In general, applicants who clearly communicate their value to employers and translate that value into an appropriate salary will be treated well on the job.

Handling Objections to Your Request

While hopefully your salary negotiation session will go smoothly and you will quickly reach agreement with the employer, many employers will raise objections to candidate's stated salary requirements. When this happens, you must be prepared to handle these objections in a positive manner that once again stresses your qualifications and benefits for the employer. This is another opportunity to be redundant about qualifications, value, performance, and benefits. Whatever objections arise, you must consistently talk about the importance of being rewarded for your **performance**. In so doing, you turn what are potentially negatives into positives that should further strengthen your position with the employer.

> *You should negotiate from a position of strength, not need or greed.*

You can expect to encounter any, or all, of these five most common salary objections:

1. Your figure is not within our budget. We can't afford to pay that much for this position.

2. Others with similar qualifications and experience don't make that much in our organization.

3. Your salary history doesn't really justify such a large salary increase.

4. This will be a tough case to argue with my boss.

5. Timing is bad because of the economy.

All of these objections to your salary request are based upon rationale unrelated to your value or performance. For example, while a **budget** always seems to be a constraint when hiring new personnel, it should not be if you have demonstrated that the employer will get a high return from your performance. Communicate your value to employers in basic cost-benefit terms – your special talents in exchange for higher performance and profits. You are an investment for greater profitability. Approaching the objection in this manner, respond to the employer by saying:

> *While I know you may have budgeted this position under $45,000, I also know many employers are willing to pay more than that. More importantly, I feel I bring to this position special skills, experience, and a commitment to performance that more than justify the $50,000.*

The rationale that you will be **paid more than others** is another non-issue for you. This is the employer's problem – not yours. What the employer pays other employees is his or her business. Your concern is that you be fairly compensated for your performance. You might respond to the employer in this manner:

> *From what you told me earlier about the importance of rewarding performance, I expected I would be offered a salary based upon my performance rather than one capped by what others make in the organization. In fact, this raises an issue that I need further clarification on: Exactly how will I be rewarded for my performance? Are raises largely a function of cost-of-living increases, or is the performance appraisal tied to yearly salary increases? I'm not sure if I understand how the compensation system operates in practice.*

The rationale that your **salary history** does not justify such a salary increase is another non-issue. You are not applying for a salary increase. Rather, you want to be compensated for the value of your work. Your salary history should have less bearing on what you receive in this position. You might respond this way:

> *I assumed I would be fairly compensated for my performance. I'm not sure how my past salary has any bearing on my work for you. In fact, I've carefully looked at this job in terms of duties and responsibilities as well as compared it to salaries in other organizations. I feel $50,000 is quite fair for what I've indicated I would achieve this first year. Would you agree that this is a fair way of arriving at this salary figure?*

As you continue to stress the performance issue in relation to compensation, you take the offensive as well as put the employer on the defensive. By taking the high road, which focuses on financially rewarding performance, you force the employer into explaining why compensation in this organization may not be related to performance. Few employers are comfortable justifying why they don't reward performance!

Receiving Benefits

Many employers will try to impress candidates with the many benefits offered by the company. These might include retirement, bonuses, stock options, medical and life insurance, child care, education reimbursement, vacations, and cost-of-living adjustments. If the employer includes these benefits in the salary negotiations, do not be overly impressed unless they translate into significant income equivalents, especially if they involve stock options that could become very valuable in the future. While benefits are important, they mainly differ **among** employers; few are negotiable with a particular employer unless you are negotiating for executive-level positions or high-demand technical positions.

Your main goal should be to negotiate for cold cash.

Except for a few employers who offer flexible benefit packages, most employers offer standard benefits – they come with the job and are equitably distributed to most employees in an organization. When negotiating salary, it is best to talk about specific dollar figures rather than get distracted by company benefits which you are likely to get anyway. It's always a good idea to negotiate the small and relatively insignificant items first but leave the most important elements, such as salary and equity participation, toward the end. Your main goal should be to negotiate for cold cash.

On the other hand, if the salary offered by the employer does not meet your expectations, but you still want the job, you could try to negotiate for some benefits which are not considered standard. These might include longer paid vacations, some flextime, and profit sharing. If the employer offers a flexible benefit package, and you receive some of the same benefits via your working spouse's compensation package, find out if some benefits with this employer can be taken in cash.

Some of the most important benefits you need to review (also see our list in Chapter 1) include the following checklist of items:

- ❑ Health, disability, and life insurance
- ❑ Reimbursement accounts
- ❑ Supplementary pay plans
- ❑ Education and training programs
- ❑ Child and day-care services
- ❑ Paid vacation time
- ❑ Unpaid leave time
- ❑ Retirement plans
- ❑ Bonuses
- ❑ Savings plans
- ❑ Professional membership dues
- ❑ Profit sharing plans
- ❑ Stock options
- ❑ 401(k) plan
- ❑ Cost-of-living adjustments
- ❑ Relocation expenses
- ❑ Perks (office, car, parking, equipment)
- ❑ Termination agreement (severance pay)

Each of these benefits involves numerous additional issues, most of which are non-negotiable. Most companies attempt to offer and administer benefits equitably. In other words, everyone within the organization receives the same benefits regardless of their position or salary. The major differences arise when comparing the benefits of one company with those of another. The benefits package in one company, for example, may be equivalent to 35 percent of your base salary, whereas in another company it may only be worth 15 percent of your salary. The differences are due to the number and extent of benefits offered by each company.

For example, insurance programs with some employers involve full coverage whereas those with other employers require some employee contribution. Retirement programs with some companies offer early-out options and a limited vested period and thus greater portability than programs with other companies that require a lengthy vesting period and limited portability. Reimbursement accounts, day-care services, and supplementary pay programs in one company may translate into a great deal of compensation for employees but these benefits may be absent in other companies.

On the other hand, some employers offer flexible benefits which present employees with **options**. These companies give employees a menu of benefit options from which to choose. If you seek employment with a company offering such options, you will have greater flexibility to structure your total compensation package. During the salary negotiation session, be sure to inquire about such options.

The Stock Option Game

Salary surveys indicate the two most important benefit issues for employees are stock options and 401(k) plans, or some form of equity or profit sharing. Stock options are especially important with start-up and high-tech companies that need an extra "competitive edge" in order to attract and keep a talented workforce in the face of traditional compensation and career advancement advantages offered by established companies. Indeed, stock options allow start-ups to create an even playing field with established companies. With stock options, venture capital, and an attractive business plan for getting rich in the future, these new companies offer a big incentive carrot, however deferred, that allows them to effectively compete from the same talent pools as well as raid the top talent of established companies.

Stock options are non-salaried financial incentives designed to offset the risky nature of these new businesses. Hiring managers in established companies increasingly see the importance of extending stock options and equity incentives to more and more categories of employees within their organization. Indeed, many employees today expect to receive such financial incentives as part of their compensation package.

Traditionally an issue most relevant to executive-level compensation, today stock options are an important compensation issue for many types and levels of employees. Indeed, the most recent trend, especially among start-up companies, has been to provide stock options to nearly all employees, from entry-level to the CEO. The reason for doing so is quite simple for employers and it follows the classic American principle of "self interest rightly understood": in a talent-driven economy with a volatile job market and high employee turnover – precipitated in part by the raiding of other companys' top talent – stock options serve the purposes of (1) motivating employees to help build a company and (2) ensuring loyalty for at least a few years. From the perspective of many employees, the purpose of stock options may be quite different: a possible road to riches should the company's stock increase substantially in value.

Stock options are one way to ensure the stability of a talented workforce which might otherwise experience high turnover if tempted by more attractive compensation packages offered by the competition. Many of the issues surrounding stock options today revolve around the number of options given to employees at different levels in an organization and defining the vesting period before one can exercise options. Typically, many organizations require four to five years before an employee becomes vested and thus can begin exercising his or her stock options. However, stock options have become so competitive that more and more companies have lowered their vesting period from four to five years to one to two years. Some companies now permit new employees to exercise 20 percent of their stock options at the end of their first year and 40 percent in each subsequent year, so an employee is literally fully vested at the end of three years.

Stock options also are an ostensible benefit creating a new type of "job lock" where employees who are either vested or about to be vested are reluctant to leave the company for greener pastures until they can cash in their options (hopefully in a market up-cycle and ideally as a new high-flying IPO). Many employers now report a new form of employee "job hopping" behavior better known as "job hedging" – employees stay around long enough to be vested and then jump ship for another company that offers a new set of generous stock options with a limited vesting period. Rather than ask about base salary and traditional benefits, many of these job applicants are mainly concerned about stock options – how many they can get and for what vested period. Not surprising, this new class of "job hedger" wants many stock options for as short a vested period possible. The primary focus of their salary negotiations is on securing stock options rather than on the base salary.

If you are applying for a job with a company that offers stock options, you should be aware of the various options available and the many issues relating to owning, purchasing, and cashing in options. Stock options can be a complicated issue involving a whole new way of thinking and talking about compensation. Different types of options, such as nonqualified stock options (NSOs), have different tax implications. For example, companies may have several types of stock options for different employees:

- incentive stock options
- nonqualified stock options
- stock grants
- common stock
- preferred stock
- restricted stock
- founders stock
- phantom stock options
- stock application rights
- stock purchase plan (discounted)

If you want to be a savvy stock option negotiator, you'll need to understand many issues relating to the new world of stock options. In so doing, you'll need to talk the language of stock options by familiarizing yourself with such concepts as vesting, strike price, capital gains, forfeit, exercise price, equity, incremental vesting, par value, shares authorized, spread, and warrants.

Renegotiate the Future

In some cases you may want a job which does not meet your immediate salary expectations. The employer may not be able to add on special benefits to satisfy you. When this happens, you might ask the employer during the interview to reconsider your salary after six months on the job. You request a six-month performance review in which your salary will be reconsidered in light of your performance. Another approach is to ask the employer to consider expanding the job description or upgrading the position and salary. Such provisions would give you time to demonstrate your value. Employers have little to lose and much to gain by agreeing to such a provision. If other negotiating approaches fail, this one is at least worth trying. At least it stresses one of your major work values – you want to be rewarded for performance.

However, you should attempt this only as a last resort. In most cases, your strongest negotiating position is always **before** you accept the job. Once hired, unless your performance is spectacular, you are not likely to receive more than the company's normal annual salary increments.

Handling Non-Negotiable Environments

Many jobs are found in organizations that do not negotiate salaries with individuals. The two major non-negotiable environments are government and companies where unions play an important role in determining compensation. In these situations, the question of salary and benefits is handled through a collective bargaining process or some other form of labor-management relations. Individuals join unions or professional groups that periodically address the compensation issue for the group as a whole. Wages and benefits are rigidly defined in order to be both equitably distributed and easily administered to everyone in the workforce. Salaries are normally assigned to qualifying levels, steps, or grades.

> *Your strongest negotiating position is always before you accept the job. Once hired, you are not likely to receive more than the company's normal annual salary increment.*

If you apply for a job with such an organization, you can expect to receive a salary and benefits assigned to the position as defined by the negotiated pay system. While individuals have little or no input into determining their salary and benefits in such systems, many individuals do manage to affect their compensation nonetheless. The major technique for negotiating in non-negotiable environments is to concentrate on the qualifications assigned to the position in order to upgrade the position. In the case of government, for example, salaries are graded according to the level of positions as defined by qualifications and experience. The lower the level of the position, the lower the salary. Therefore, if you want to move into the higher levels of the salary scale, you must have the qualifications and experience required for positions at those levels. Negotiating in this environment involves concentrating on the qualifications for positions.

You have two options here. First, you can **redefine your qualifications** so they meet the requirements of the higher-level positions. You do this by carefully analyzing the qualifications specified for the position as well as your own background. Try to match the two as closely as possible. If you are interested in working for the federal government, for example, some agencies may even help you rewrite your application so it best meets the qualifications specified for the position. In so doing, you may receive a higher salary than you would have had you not had such agency assistance. The key to getting a high rating is how you describe your knowledge, skills, abilities, and other characteristics (KSAO factors).

> *Many employers are reluctant to negotiate salaries upwards prior to seeing you perform in their organization.*

In the second option, you might persuade the employer to **create a new position** which will be defined around your qualifications. Widely practiced in government and other organizations, this is called "wiring" a position. An employer who wants to hire a particular individual literally writes a new position description around the qualifications of the individual. The position is defined at the salary level, step, or grade that is acceptable to the candidate being hired.

Don't Expect Too Much

Many applicants have unrealistic salary expectations and exaggerated notions of their worth to potential employers. Some occupational groups, such as postal and auto workers, appear overpaid for the type of skills they use and the quality of the work they produce. In recent years several unions began renegotiating contracts in a new direction – downwards. Unions gave back salary increases and benefits won in previous years in order to maintain job security in the face of deepening job loss and recessions. Workers in many industries were not in a position to further increase their salaries. Many employers believed salaries had become extremely inflated in relation to profits. Such

Negotiate the Best Compensation Package 137

salaries, in turn, created even more inflated salary expectations among job hunters. A similar situation occurs in many start-up companies that face difficult financial situations after a year or two of operations. Many of the troubled firms renegotiate compensation with the result that many employees take significant salary cuts as well as lower expectations about "getting rich" on stock options. Many employees become "job hedgers" as they cut their losses and move on to other similar firms that offer perhaps more promising stock options.

Given the declining power of unions, turbulent economic conditions, the increased prevalence of "give-back" schemes, and greater emphasis on productivity and performance in the workplace, many employers are reluctant to negotiate salaries upwards prior to seeing you perform in their organization. Many also prefer rewarding employees with incentive pay and performance bonuses rather than inflate salary bases. In a tight job market, many employers feel they can maintain their ground on salary offers. After all, as more well qualified candidates glut the job market, employers know they are in a buyer's market. And candidates confirm the wisdom of employers – they are willing to accept lower salaries in exchange for job security. In a seller's market, job seekers can negotiate more compensation in the form of benefits, which are often used by employers to attract candidates.

> *If you can't translate your salary expectations into dollars-and-cents profits for the employer, perhaps you shouldn't be negotiating at all!*

Given this situation, you may find it increasingly difficult to negotiate higher salaries with employers who have little or no incentive to haggle over money. If you plan to negotiate, be prepared to stress your special value to the employer. You must clearly communicate how you will benefit the employer. You'll need to talk in the employer's language of **benefits**. You'll have to make a hard sale, complete with evidence of past performance and examples of what you plan to accomplish in the future. For example, if you think you are worth $50,000 a year, will you be productive enough to generate $300,000 of business for the company to justify that amount? If you can't translate your salary expectations into dollars-and-cents profits for the employer, perhaps you shouldn't be negotiating at all! You might be more comfortable doing what most other job seekers do – accept what's initially offered, with no questions asked.

9

Finalize the Offer With Attitude

YOUR JOB OFFER IS not complete until you finalize the salary question. Once you reach a verbal agreement concerning compensation, you still need to do several things before starting the new job. How you handle this period may affect how well you get along on the job.

Take Time

Once an employer offers you a job, you may want to ask for time to think it over. Ask to consider it for a day or two. A common professional courtesy is to give you at least 48 hours to assess an offer. During this time, you may want to carefully examine the job and consider other important questions at this stage:

- Is it worth what I am being offered?
- Can I do better?
- What are other employers offering for comparable positions?

If one or two other employers are considering you for a job, let this employer know his or her job is not the only one under consideration; you may be in demand elsewhere. This should give you a better bargaining position. Contact the other employers and let them know you have a job offer and that you would like to have your application status with them clarified before you make any decisions with the other employer. Depending on how much flexibility an employer may have to accelerate a hiring decision, you may be able to go back to the first employer with another job offer. With a second job offer in hand, you may greatly enhance your bargaining position.

> *With a second job offer in hand, you may greatly enhance your bargaining position.*

Consider the Offer

The job offer involves much more than a general invitation or commitment to hire you. If and when the employer says *"We want you to join our team"* or *"You're hired,"* you still need to work out the details of your employment. At the very least, these details should include four major components:

- Your specific duties and responsibilities.

- Expectations of your performance during the next year.

- A compensation package.

- A provision for reviewing both your performance and compensation.

You need to reach a mutual understanding about these important points that will affect your job. For example, both you and the employer should have a clear understanding of what exactly you will be doing in this job. Think of **duties** and **responsibilities** as your inputs into the company – things you are expected to do on a day-to-day basis. If you don't know what your duties and responsibilities are, you may quickly discover the nature of the job changes. You may be expected to do many things you were never hired to do or things that have little to do with your strengths. Such a situation could become disastrous as you begin demonstrating your weaknesses rather than your strengths. Therefore, it's best to clarify your job duties and responsibilities at this point so that there will be no misunderstanding.

You also need to settle the issue of **performance**. What exactly are you expected to achieve during the first year? Does the employer have certain goals in mind for this position that can be clearly identified and measured? For example, are you expected to reorganize a section, increase markets and improve profits by a certain percentage, produce a certain number of reports, or represent the company at seven different meetings? Think of performance in terms of outputs or outcomes.

Knowing your duties and responsibilities and understanding what performance is expected from you are only the first steps in completing the job offer. More importantly, you also need to know how performance is both **measured** and **rewarded**. For example, does the employer conduct annual performance reviews? If so, how are they conducted? What assessment are used? Does it involve a self-evaluation along with a peer and supervisory evaluation? What input will you have in the evaluation process? What other types of evaluations take place? For example, are nonproductivity evaluations used in determining raises and promotions?

> *Think of performance in terms of outputs or outcomes.*

At the same time, is the compensation system directly linked to the evaluation system? If the employer tells you that in this company performance is important and is rewarded, then the employer needs to spell out exactly how the system operates in practice. Ask for specifics. For example, when does the performance evaluation takes place? If the process begins in, for example, April, when does it conclude and what final form does it take? Do you meet with your supervisor for feedback and for setting goals for the coming year, or is this an impersonal and secretive process just between your supervisor and his or her boss? Are raises and promotions largely a function of seniority or directly related to the performance evaluation?

These and other questions should be answered prior to accepting any job offer. If not, these questions may soon arise on the job and the answers may well disappoint you. At that time, you will lament the fact that you did not seek clarification on how the employer's personnel and compensation systems operated.

Get It in Writing

Talk is cheap, and it often leads to misunderstandings if not put into writing. Questions of duties and responsibilities, expected performance, evaluations, and compensation lie at the heart of any job. These are important questions that require some form of written agreement and commitment on the part of the employer.

Verbal agreements may be okay between close and trusted friends, but they don't have much weight in employment situations. After all, the company representative who made verbal agreements with you may be gone tomorrow, and he or she most likely will not share the commitments with the person taking his or her place. Verbal agreements that are important to you and your job should always be put into writing. You can start doing this by taking notes during the salary negotiation session. At some point, preferably near the end, when you are expected to either accept or decline the offer, ask the employer to summarize your verbal agreement. As this is being done, write down each point. When he or she finishes summarizing the agreement, read back the agreement as you have written it down in your notes. And then end by saying,

> *This is my understanding of what I will be expected to do as well as my compensation. Is this correct?*

Assuming the employer agrees, you should next ask if he or she could put this agreement in writing:

> *I would appreciate it if you could put this all in writing within the next two days. In addition to putting a copy in my personnel file, I would like a copy for my own files. I would appreciate if we would use this agreement as the basis for conducting a six-month performance appraisal. I think that might be a good time to evaluate my work and to make sure we are going in the right direction with this job.*

If the employer has not been taking similar notes, make a copy for his or her reference. And make sure that the final written agreement indeed conforms to your notes and that it is completed within two days. You want this agreement in writing prior to quitting your present job and starting this new job.

Accept, Close, and Follow Through

Once you have a verbal agreement about the terms of your employment as well as an indication that your agreement will be put into writing within the next two days, you should accept the offer in both a professional and personal manner.

Assuming you have negotiated in a professional manner and both you and the employer are satisfied with the agreement, it is now time to set the stage for starting the job. At this point you want to make sure you are starting this job on the right foot. The employer now has certain performance expectations which are tied to the salary you negotiated. The employer will be carefully observing you over the next few months in hopes of confirming that he or she made the right hiring and compensation decisions. You do not want to disappoint the employer.

At the conclusion of the salary negotiation session, reassure the employer that he or she made the correct decision. You can do this by restating your interest in the job, your delight in joining the organization, and your commitment to performance. You want to express an important **attitude** here that should continue on the job. You might conclude by saying something like the following – but in your own words:

> *It's been a pleasure meeting and working with you on this position. I've been very impressed with the professional manner in which you have conducted the interviews and extended the job offer. I'm very much looking forward to joining you and your staff. This is the type of organization I believe is ideally suited for my long-term interests and skills. I'm very anxious to begin working on the new marketing plan for expanding our sales into Hong Kong and Manila. This is an area I've worked in for years, and I'm confident we will see some major progress here. Thank you for your trust.*

After leaving this session, you should follow up your acceptance of the job offer with a nice thank-you letter in which you reiterate the same points you made at the conclusion of the salary negotiation session. This is a thoughtful and courteous thing to do. Employers tend to remember such thoughtful gestures in a positive manner. Such a letter may well set a very positive tone for future compensation discussions with this employer. It may be one of the most important letters you ever address to your employer. An example of a thoughtful follow-up thank-you letter appears on page 145.

Job Offer Acceptance

7694 James Court
San Francisco, CA 94826
January 23, 19____

Judith Green
Vice President
West Coast Airlines
2400 Van Ness
San Francisco, CA 94829

Dear Ms. Green:

I am pleased to be joining your organization and am looking forward to meeting you and your staff again next month.

The customer relations position is ideally suited to my background and interests. I assure you I will give you my best effort in making this an effective position within your company.

I understand I will begin work on February 21. If, in the meantime, I need to complete any paperwork or take care of any other matters, please contact me.

I enjoyed meeting with you and your staff and appreciated the very professional manner in which the hiring was conducted.

Sincerely,

Joan Kitner

Joan Kitner

10

Salary Increases, Raises, and Promotions

MANY OF THE PRINCIPLES we outlined for dealing with salary during the job search are equally valid for negotiating salary increases once you are on the job. Some organizations conduct annual salary reviews whereas others deal with salaries and raises on an ad hoc basis. Depending on the type of organization you work for, you may be involved in an annual salary review process where a performance appraisal is linked to raises. On the other hand, you may work for an organization where raises are largely determined by annual cost-of-living increases or employee organizations, such as collective bargaining units, that negotiate higher wages and benefits. Patterns vary from one organization to another.

The Myth of Performance

Performance is important to employers and organizations. However, one must also be realistic about how performance is recognized, rewarded, and promoted. To just do a good job is not enough. You must communicate to others that you are a producer who gets things done for the group and organization.

At the same time, performance is one of those wonderful terms like "efficiency" and "honesty." Almost everyone agrees it is important, but few do much about it. While many employers give lip service to performance, they actually reward people on the basis of seniority, inflation, and politics.

Performance is only one of many criteria for rewarding employees. It may or may not be the most important criterion compared to other on-the-job considerations. Therefore, if you want salary increases and promotions, you must understand how the personnel system operates in both theory and practice. It will vary from one organization to another. In some organizations it operates according to the book: rewards are dispensed through the operation of an objective performance appraisal system. In other organizations it operates according to Byzantine bureaucratic politics – the ebb and flow of power, influence, and intrigue. Whom you know and how you play the game of organizational politics will largely determine your raises and promotions.

Just because employers say that performance is important in personnel decisions is no reason to believe they reward performance.

Just because employers say that performance is important in personnel decisions is no reason to believe they reward performance. Unfortunately, you really won't know how the reward system operates until you become part of the organization.

Indeed, it would be naive for us to suggest the reality of most organizations is that they put performance first. If they did, fewer companies would fail and most would do much better than they do at present. Most organizations are more or less "performance oriented," depending on the internal structure of power and personnel. The reality is that you must work with people as well as with things and processes. While your performance may center around how well you work with things, your rewards will be dispensed by how well you work with the people who have power. Consequently, once on the job, you must take particular care of how well you deal with those who are important to your future. This may mean attaching yourself to a mentor who, in turn, sponsors you within the organization. In other words, it means sucking up to power and being a team player.

While all workers may enter the organization with similar qualifications and experience, those who get ahead do so because they do things differently from others. What they do differently is much more than just performance. They also network their way to job and career success by being in the right place at the right time and with the right set of sponsors and promoters.

Nonetheless, your most important asset in getting ahead will be your performance. Focus on performance, but make sure it gets communicated to the right people who have the power to dispense rewards.

Get Performance Raises

Most employees receive raises on the basis of cost-of-living increases, performance criteria, bonuses, or promotions. Being incremental, most such increases are figured as a percentage of one's present salary base – 3 to 8 percent. Few employees receive major salary increases – 10 to 30 percent – other than those which come with promotions or major bonuses. In other words, they must change jobs within the organization in order to significantly boost their earnings. Therefore, your initial starting salary will be the major determiner of your future salaries with your present employer – unless you do something different from other employees.

> *Focus on performance, but make sure it gets communicated to the right people who have the power to dispense rewards.*

Ideally, everyone should be rewarded on the basis of their work performance. But in reality it is very difficult for employers to measure performance, because they often lack a performance appraisal system that would define jobs in terms of performance criteria. In addition, performance appraisals have a tendency to become politicized within organizations. They may create more internal conflicts and turmoil than they are worth.

In the end, many employers prefer giving everyone across-the-board increases – despite individual performance differences – rather than get involved in the politics of performance appraisals. Principles of equity and ease of administration often override such values as individual fairness when dealing with the issue of who gets how much of a raise this year. Not surprisingly, employers often lack a clear idea of what they want in a new employee since they have not tied performance criteria nor a per-

Salary Increases, Raises, and Promotions 149

formance appraisal system to the issue of compensation. Their preference for using salary history and comparative salary figures in justifying salaries is a further indication that they have not dealt with the critical issue of performance in the workplace.

If you work in an organization that uses an annual salary review process to determine raises, it's best to approach such a process the same way in which you would approach the salary negotiation when applying for a job. The key to making this process work in your favor is to **document your performance**. If a performance appraisal is central to the annual salary review, know what the performance criteria are and make sure you have been documenting your accomplishments throughout the year. In addition to the performance appraisal form used by the employer, you should keep a **diary of your accomplishments**. This might be in the form of a notebook in which you make entries at the end of each day or week. Include the following categories of information in your performance diary:

1. **Achievements:** Those things that resulted in some type of improvement to your job or organization, such as efficiency, effectiveness, and profitability.

2. **Problems solved:** Demonstrates your abilities and responsiveness to the needs of the organization.

3. **New initiatives taken:** Documents initiative and added value to the organization.

4. **Additional duties and responsibilities performed outside your job description:** Indicates an expansion of your job for which you should receive additional rewards.

Avoid the tendency to document activities or workload statistics, many of which are routines that produce few measurable outcomes or accomplishments. You want to focus on those things that are more likely to be rewarded by employers – outcomes, results, or benefits. Instead of stating

Completed three 30-page reports in two weeks

restate this workload statistic – which is consistent with your assigned duties and responsibilities – as a specific outcome or benefit for the employer:

Completed three critical and time-sensitive 30-page reports that resulted in a 25-percent increase in funding for Project Ready Start.

In addition, you want to achieve a certain degree of **visibility** within the organization that communicates to your supervisor and his or her boss your value as well as your positive attitudes and behaviors. You do this through meetings, memos, and recognition through others. For example, you should keep your supervisor informed about what you are achieving. If you manage to acquire a new client or conclude a major sale, write a memo to your supervisor in which you document this achievement. If you receive recognition or praise from a customer or colleague relevant to your job, send a copy to your supervisor. When you attend meetings in which your supervisor is in attendance, make sure to contribute with intelligent questions and suggestions. As you continue to communicate value and performance to the employer, you want to build a reputation as someone who is good at what he or she does; you have the right attitude and you are reliable, trustworthy, and likable. Such interpersonal communications should reinforce the written documentation you assemble in your performance diary as well as the information contained in your memos.

> *Find successful people you admire and attach yourself to them.*

You should also **build networks** with mentors in the organization. Find successful people you admire and attach yourself to them for the purpose of better performing your job and learning how the organization operates. Ask them for advice on doing your job and moving up the organizational ladder. Let them know that you want to get ahead. While you want to be rewarded as a performer, you must also be realistic in terms of how rewards are dispensed within the organization. One of the best ways of getting your performance recognized and rewarded is to have a sponsor who takes a personal interest in seeing you move ahead.

Taking Salary Initiative

If you feel you are being under-compensated for your present level of work, you should do something about this problem. If you are not likely to be promoted to a higher paying job and salary raises are largely non-negotiable within your present organization, you might start looking for another employer. After all, your best salary will probably be the one you initially negotiate with your next employer. Begin conducting a job search but do so discreetly. Avoid applying for jobs that appear to be blind ads. Your present employer could be behind such an ad, and it could be your position they are advertising! There is no better way of losing your value in the eyes of your present employer than for him or her to find out that you are indiscreetly looking for another job.

Your best salary will probably be the one you negotiate with your next employer.

However, most employers have some flexibility to negotiate salary with their employees. Assuming you have gathered comparable salary data, documented your performance, and regularly communicated your performance to the employer, you should be in a strong position to talk with him or her frankly about your salary. Again, approach this issue from the employer's perspective rather than from a self-centered perspective of need, greed, or self-esteem. If your needs are much above a salary that your present position can justify, you should focus your attention on a promotion rather than a salary raise; a new salary should automatically come with a new position. In addition to stressing your performance in your present job, you will need to convince the employer that you will also do well in a new position. Approach this discussion the same way you would a job interview. After all, you will be interviewing for a new job rather than just a salary raise. The difference is that the employer is already familiar with you as both a person and a professional.

When you speak with your employer about a raise or promotion, you should focus on why you deserve the money or position. Use supports to justify your request. Expect the employer to raise the same objections you would encounter during a job interview: budgetary limitations, company profits are down, the economy looks shaky, others don't make that much, and your salary history doesn't justify such an increase. Deal with these objections in the same manner as you would during the salary negotiation session of the job interview: focus on your value, but this time give examples of performance relevant to this employer and the organization.

Threats and Alternative Offers

As a bargaining tool, threatening to quit unless your salary and promotion demands are met is a very risky, high stakes business. Never threaten to quit unless you really mean it. When given an ultimatum by an employee, many employers will thank the employee for his or her good work and then politely show them the door. Unless you are so instrumental to the functioning of the organization – and few if any people are – this negotiating tactic is likely to backfire.

You must be prepared to do what you say you will do. And that means having an alternative job offer. Threatening to quit without such an offer is an invitation to self-induced unemployment!

Never threaten to quit unless you really mean it.

On the other hand, if you have an alternative job offer, you should be in the strongest position to renegotiate your salary or discuss a promotion. Prepare a list of those things you would need in order to stay with this organization. Your discussion will be less focused on your performance than on what the employer needs to do in order to keep you. If the employer really wants you to stay, he or she should be able to find the money for a raise or the means to promote you.

If you unexpectedly submit your resignation, because you already accepted a job offer with another employer, your present employer may try to persuade you to stay by sweetening your compensation package as well as offering you a promotion. If your present employer offers you a deal you can't refuse, you might be better off staying where you are, since you have substantially increased your value in the eyes of this employer. On the other hand, the new employer might feel deceived, since it appears you used him or her as leverage for getting a promotion and raise. You might also go back to the new employer and share your new problem: your present employer is offering you a better position and compensation package than this employer. While sensitive and somewhat embarrassing for some people, this is the type of problem many employees wish they encountered more often. Just make sure you don't alienate both employers in the process of bargaining for a better position and more compensation. You could very well find yourself burning both ends of the candle while holding it in the middle!

For more information and tips on getting a raise, see our companion salary raise and promotion volume, which is specifically designed for individuals who want to get ahead with their current employer: *Get a Raise in 7 Days: 10 Salary Savvy Steps to Success* (Manassas Park, VA: Impact Publications).

11

Salary Finder

IDENTIFYING SALARY RANGES for particular jobs is relatively easy given numerous studies that survey salaries. However, the more you learn about salary ranges, the more elusive this information seems for particular situations and the less useful it becomes for individual decision-making.

Salaries and Salary Ranges

The basic problem with salary surveys is that most are conducted on a national or regional level for general types of positions. However, individuals work in specific positions, for particular organizations, within specific communities, and at different skill and experience levels. While national and regional salary information may give you a general idea of the high and low salaries for certain types of jobs, they do so only in the aggregate. Furthermore, salary surveys tend to be inconsistent.

If you want to determine salary ranges appropriate for a particular position, you need to consult several publications, which primarily present data compiled by the U.S. Department of Labor and other state and local government sources. We recommend starting with Joyce P. Simkin (ed.) ***American Salaries and Wages Survey*** (Farmington Hills, MI: Gale Cengage Learning, 2007). This volume presents more than 300 data sources for more than 42,000 salaries in 4,500+ occupational classifications in hundreds of cities throughout the nation. A new salary directory, *Salary Facts Handbook* (JIST Publishing, 2008), includes salary information on 800 jobs. The Department of Labor's biannual *Occupational Outlook Handbook* includes salary information on 270 major occupations. Also, check out Michael Farr's and Laurence Shatkin's *250 Best-Paying Jobs* (JIST Publishing, 2007), which includes much of the same U.S. Department of Labor salary data that appears in the other directories and handbooks.

For the most current and accurate information on salary ranges, consult the U.S. Department of Labor's *Area Wage Surveys* and *White-Collar Pay: Private Service-Producing Industries*. The *Area Wage Surveys* include data from 188 surveys of metropolitan areas which are conducted annually and biannually. Produced by the Bureau of Labor Statistics, these Department of Labor publications are available through the U.S. Government Printing Office and at several major libraries.

Most major **trade and professional associations** also have information on current salary ranges for particular positions. Names, addresses, and phone numbers of these associations are listed in the latest editions of the *Occupational Outlook Handbook* (Washington, DC: U.S. Department of Labor), *Encyclopedia of Associations* (Farmington Hills: Gale Cengage Learning), *National Trade and Professional Associations* (Washington, DC: Columbia Books), and *Associations USA* (Detroit: Omnigraphics).

Most **state employment offices** keep data of salary ranges for occupations in your local area. If you have any questions, please call your local employment office and ask them if they have any data of salary ranges for your particular occupational area of interest. Many of these offices keep national, state, and local salary range data for thousands of jobs. Most state labor offices periodically conduct wage surveys for thousands of positions.

Graduating college students should consult the annual *Salary Survey*, published by the National Association of Colleges and Employers (NACE) in Bethlehem, Pennsylvania, which includes salary ranges for hundreds of entry-level positions for college graduates. For example, the average salaries offered in summer 2007 for candidates with these selected majors were as follows:

- Chemical Engineering — $59,361
- Computer Engineering — $56,201
- Electrical Engineering — $55,292
- Mechanical Engineering — $54,128
- Computer Science — $53,396
- Civil Engineering — $48,509
- Economics — $48,483
- Management of Information Systems — $47,648
- Finance — $47,239
- Accounting — $46,718
- Business Administration/Management — $43,701
- Marketing — $40,161
- Political Science/Government — $34,590
- History — $33,768
- English — $32,553
- Sociology — $32,033
- Psychology — $31,631

Contact the career center at your local college and university to review a copy of this publication. Most career centers should have a copy of this definitive survey

Many newly minted MBAs from top graduate schools (Stanford, Harvard, Wharton, Kellogg) now command six-figure starting salaries with major corporations. For example, Bloomberg.com reported that the average compensation package (includes signing bonuses and other benefits) for June 2007 graduates of the Harvard Business School's MBA program was worth $174,580.

Numerous companies, such as the Economic Research Institute (www.erieri.com), SalarySource (www.salarysource.com), Robert Half International (www.rhii.com), and Abbott, Langer, and Associates (www.abbott-langer.com) also periodically conduct salary surveys. Private employment agencies and executive search firms usually have accurate information on salary ranges for hundreds of jobs for which they recruit. Much of these data can be found by reviewing these two websites: JobStar (www.jobstar.org) and Salary.com (www.salary.com).

Local Variations

While salary surveys provide you with useful nationwide and regional data, the problem with most studies is that they may not be relevant to your particular situation. Different communities, organizations, and employers can account for as much as 40 percent variation in average

Salary Finder 157

salaries. If, for example, you plan to work in Cedar Rapids, Iowa as a word processor, you can expect to make 30 percent less than if you worked as a word processor in San Francisco, California.

You will have to take wage and salary studies one or two levels further as you focus on particular communities, organizations, and employers. In other words, you need to think nationally but act locally when dealing with salary and salary ranges. Examine these salary surveys for general guidelines, but do not take them as accurate reflections of the salary structure for positions in your community or the organization you are applying to or in which you work at present. To get accurate information on salaries at this level, you will have to conduct your own salary survey as we outlined in Chapter 4.

Take, for example, salaries for dental assistants. According to the U.S. Department of Labor's salary estimates for May 2006 (see *Salary Facts Handbook*), the salary range for dental assistants was $20,530 to $43,040, depending on the industry and location and where the job was part-time or full-time. Dental assistants averaged the following annual salaries in these top 30 metropolitan areas:

> *You need to think nationally but act locally when dealing with salaries and salary ranges.*

- Atlanta, GA $32,160
- Baltimore, MD $32,110
- Boston, MA $36,390
- Chicago, IL $30,710
- Cincinnati, OH $32,050
- Cleveland, OH $28,180
- Columbus, OH $31,060
- Dallas, TX $28,940
- Denver, CO $35,170
- Detroit, MI $32,220
- Houston, TX $23,240
- Kansas City, MO $29,530
- Las Vegas, NV $33,420
- Los Angeles, CA $29,910
- Miami, FL $28,800
- Minneapolis, MN $38,840
- New York City, NY $32,880
- Orlando, FL $32,810
- Philadelphia, PA $30,400

- Phoenix, AZ $33,250
- Pittsburgh, PA $25,930
- Portland, OR $35,370
- Riverside, CA $28,190
- Sacramento, CA $35,110
- San Diego, CA $33,600
- San Francisco, CA $34,730
- Seattle, WA $36,840
- Tampa, FL $29,170
- St. Louis, MO $28,410
- Washington, DC $33,520

You will discover salary ranges for all occupations will vary from one community to another. Again, it's important to conduct your own local salary research rather than rely on highly generalized salary ranges from nationwide data which may be 2-4 years old.

Salaries for 795 Selected Occupations

According the U.S. Department of Labor's 2006 salary projections as presented in the *Salary Facts Handbook*, the median annual earnings for 795 selected jobs include the following:

Rank	Title	Median Earnings
1.	Anesthesiologists	$145,600+
2.	Chief Executives	$145,600+
3.	Family and General Practitioners	$145,600+
4.	Internists, General	$145,600+
5.	Obstetricians and Gynecologists	$145,600+
6.	Oral and Maxillofacial Surgeons	$145,600+
7.	Orthodontists	$145,600+
8.	Physicians and Surgeons, All Other	$145,600+
9.	Prosthodontists	$145,600+
10.	Psychiatrists	$145,600+
11.	Surgeons	$145,600+
12.	Airline Pilots, Copilots, and Flight Engineers	$141,090
13.	Pediatricians, General	$138,130
14.	Dentists, General	$132,140
15.	Air Traffic Controllers	$117,240
16.	Podiatrists	$108,220
17.	Engineering Managers	$105,430
18.	Lawyers	$102,470
19.	Judges, Magistrate Judges, and Magistrates	$101,690
20.	Computer and Information Systems Managers	$101,580

21.	Natural Sciences Managers	$100,080
22.	Marketing Managers	$98,720
23.	Petroleum Engineers	$98,380
24.	Astronomers	$95,740
25.	Pharmacists	$94,520
26.	Physicists	$94,240
27.	Computer and Information Scientists, Research	$93,950
28.	Sales Managers	$91,560
29.	Dentists, All Other Specialists	$91,200
30.	Optometrists	$91,040
31.	Financial Managers	$90,970
32.	Nuclear Engineers	$90,220
33.	Political Scientists	$90,140
34.	Human Resources Managers, All Other	$88,510
35.	Computer Hardware Engineers	$88,470
36.	Aerospace Engineers	$87,610
37.	Law Teachers, Postsecondary	$87,240
38.	Mathematicians	$88,930
39.	Industrial-Organizational Psychologists	$86,420
40.	Computer Software Engineers, Systems Software	$85,370
41.	General and Operations Managers	$85,230
42.	Physical Scientists, All Other	$83,450
43.	Actuaries	$82,800
44.	Managers, All Other	$82,490
45.	Public Relations Managers	$82,180
46.	Engineers, All Others	$81,660
47.	Purchasing Managers	$81,570
48.	Electronics Engineers, Except Computer	$81,050
49.	Training and Development Managers	$80,250
50.	Computer and Software Engineers, Applications	$79,780
51.	Chemical Engineers	$78,860
52.	Education Administrators, Elementary and Secondary School	$77,740
53.	Sales Engineers	$77,720
54.	Industrial Production Managers	$77,670
55.	Health Specialties Teachers, Postsecondary	$77,190
56.	Atmospheric and Space Scientists	$77,150
57.	Economists	$77,010
58.	Engineering Teachers, Postsecondary	$76,670
59.	Biochemists and Biophysicists	$76,320
60.	Psychologists, All Other	$76,310
61.	Electrical Engineers	$75,930
62.	Agricultural Sciences Teachers, Postsecondary	$75,140
63.	Physician Assistants	$74,980
64.	Compensation and Benefits Managers	$74,750
65.	Materials Scientists	$74,610
66.	Education Administrators, Postsecondary	$73,990

67.	Materials Engineers	$73,990
68.	Biomedical Engineers	$73,930
69.	Construction Managers	$73,700
70.	Medical and Health Services Managers	$73,340
71.	Transportation, Storage, and Distribution Managers	$73,080
72.	Advertising and Promotions Managers	$73,060
73.	Marine Engineers and Naval Architects	$72,990
74.	Geoscientists, Except Hydrologists and Geographers	$72,660
75.	Administrative Law Judges, Adjudicators, and Hearing Officers	$72,660
76.	Mining and Geological Engineers, Including Mining Safety Engineers	$72,160
77.	Veterinarians	$71,990
78.	Economics Teachers, Postsecondary	$71,850
79.	Environmental Engineers	$69,940
80.	Mechanical Engineers	$69,850
81.	Computer Systems Analysts	$69,760
82.	Nuclear Power Reactor Operators	$69,370
83.	First-Line Supervisors/Managers of Police and Detectives	$69,310
84.	Atmospheric, Earth, Marine and Space Sciences Teachers, Postsecondary	$69,300
85.	Biological Science Teachers, Postsecondary	$69,210
86.	Industrial Engineers	$68,620
87.	Civil Engineers	$68,600
88.	Computer Specialists, All Other	$68,570
89.	Securities, Commodities, and Financial Services Sales Agents	$68,500
90.	Physics Teachers, Postsecondary	$68,170
91.	Art Directors	$68,100
92.	Management Analysts	$68,050
93.	Administrative Services Managers	$67,690
94.	Education Administrators, All Other	$66,620
95.	Financial Analysts	$66,590
96.	Health and Safety Engineers, Except Mining Safety Engineers and Inspectors	$66,290
97.	Hydrologists	$66,260
98.	Physical Therapists	$66,200
99.	Radiation Therapists	$66,170
100.	Personal Financial Advisors	$66,120
101.	Agricultural Engineers	$66,030
102.	Statisticians	$65,720
103.	Computer Programmers	$65,510
104.	First-Line Supervisors/Managers of Non-Retail Sales Workers	$65,510
105.	Nuclear Technicians	$65,500
106.	Financial Examiners	$65,370

107.	Chiropractors	$65,220
108.	Social Scientists and Related Workers, All Other	$64,920
109.	Environmental Science Teachers, Postsecondary	$94,780
110.	Database Administrators	$64,670
111.	Operations Research Analysts	$64,650
112.	Architecture Teachers, Postsecondary	$64,620
113.	Network Systems and Date Communications Analysts	$64,600
114.	Agents and Business Managers of Artists, Performers, and Athletes	$64,500
115.	Sales Representatives, Wholesale and Manufacturing, Technical and Scientific Products	$64,440
116.	Forestry and Conservation Science Teachers, Postsecondary	$64,430
117.	Architects, Except Landscape and Navel	$64,150
118.	Postsecondary Teachers, All Other	$63,930
119.	Elevator Installers and Repairers	$63,620
120.	Mathematical Scientists, All Other	$63,570
121.	Logisticians	$63,430
122.	Geographers	$62,990
123.	First-Line Supervisors/Managers of Fire Fighting and Prevention Workers	$62,900
124.	Anthropology and Archeology Teachers, Postsecondary	$62,820
125.	Gaming Managers	$62,820
126.	Dental Hygienists	$62,800
127.	Fashion Designers	$62,610
128.	Power Distributors and Dispatchers	$62,590
129.	Nuclear Medicine Technologists	$62,300
130.	Network and Computer Systems Administrators	$62,130
131.	Business Teachers, Postsecondary	$62,040
132.	Political Science Teachers, Postsecondary	$61,820
133.	Medical Scientists, Except Epidemiologists	$61,680
134.	Health Diagnosing and Treating Practitioners, All Other	$61,570
135.	Budget Analysts	$61,430
136.	Chemistry Teachers, Postsecondary	$61,220
137.	Social Sciences Teachers, Postsecondary, All Other	$61,210
138.	Biological Scientists, All Other	$60,940
139.	Real Estate Brokers	$60,790
140.	Occupational Therapists	$60,470
141.	Sociologists	$60,290
142.	Chemists	$59,870
143.	Clinical, Counseling, and School Psychologists	$59,440
144.	Geography Teachers, Postsecondary	$59,000
145.	Orthotists and Prosthetists	$58,980
146.	Market Research Analysts	$58,820

147.	Psychology Teachers, Postsecondary	$58,670
148.	Detectives and Criminal Investigators	$58,260
149.	Technical Writers	$58,050
150.	Occupational Health and Safety Specialists	$58,030
151.	Locomotive Engineers	$57,990
152.	Microbiologists	$57,980
153.	Speech-Language Pathologists	$57,710
154.	Computer Science Teachers, Postsecondary	$57,620
155.	Commercial Pilots	$57,480
156.	Electrical and Electronics Repairers, Powerhouse, Substation, and Relay	$57,400
157.	History Teachers, Postsecondary	$57,390
158.	Registered Nurses	$57,280
159.	Diagnostic Medical Sonographers	$57,160
160.	Audiologists	$57,120
161.	Life Scientists, All Other	$56,970
162.	Epidemiologists	$56,670
163.	Urban and Regional Planners	$56,630
164.	Sociology Teachers, Postsecondary	$56,620
165.	Mathematical Science Teachers, Postsecondary	$56,420
166.	Area, Ethnic, and Cultural Studies Teachers, Postsecondary	$56,380
167.	Producers and Directors	$56,310
168.	Environmental Scientists and Specialists, Including Health	$56,100
169.	Social and Plate Scientists	$56,080
170.	Postmasters and Mail Superintendents	$55,790
171.	Business Operations Specialists, All Other	$55,650
172.	Railroad Conductors and Yardmasters	$55,530
173.	Home Economics Teachers, Postsecondary	$55,310
174.	Nursing Instructors and Teachers, Postsecondary	$55,280
175.	Landscape Architects	$55,140
176.	Power Plant Operators	$55,000
177.	Conservation Scientists	$54,970
178.	Philosophy and Religion Teachers, Postsecondary	$54,880
179.	Ship Engineers	$54,820
180.	Accountants and Auditors	$54,630
181.	Library Science Teachers, Postsecondary	$54,570
182.	Commercial and Industrial Designers	$54,560
183.	Social Work Teachers, Postsecondary	$54,340
184.	Engineering Technicians, Except Drafters, All Other	$54,250
185.	First-Line Supervisors/Managers of Mechanics, Installers, and Repairers	$53,890
186.	First-Line Supervisors/Managers of Construction Trades and Extraction Workers	$53,850
187.	Food Scientists and Technologists	$53,810
188.	Flight Attendants	$53,780

Salary Finder 163

189.	Financial Specialists, All Other	$53,680
190.	Gas Plant Operators	$53,670
191.	Captains, Mates, and Pilots of Water Vessels	$53,430
192.	Aerospace Engineering and Operations Technicians	$53,300
193.	Zoologists and Wildlife Biologists	$53,300
194.	Art, Drama, and Music Teachers, Postsecondary	$53,160
195.	Communications Teachers, Postsecondary	$53,110
196.	Cost Estimators	$52,940
197.	Education Teachers, Postsecondary	$52,800
198.	Instructional Coordinators	$52,790
199.	First-Line Supervisors/Managers of Correctional Officers	$52,580
200.	Telecommunications Equipment Installers and Repairers, Except Line Installers	$52,430
201.	Petroleum Pump System Operators, Refinery Operators and Gaugers	$52,380
202.	Credit Analysts	$52,350
203.	Insurance Underwriters	$52,350
204.	Human Resources, Training, and Labor Relations Specialists, All Other	$52,270
205.	Farm, Ranch, and Other Agricultural Managers	$52,070
206.	Media and Communication Equipment Workers All Others	$52,070
207.	Social and Community Service Managers	$52,070
208.	Foreign Language and Literature Teachers, Postsecondary	$52,900
209.	Loan Officers	$51,900
210.	English Language and Literature Teachers, Postsecondary	$51,730
211.	Multi-Media Artists and Animators	$51,350
213.	Electrical Power-Line Installers and Repairers	$50,580
214.	Purchasing Agents, Except Wholesale, Retail, and Farm Products	$50,730
215.	Claims Adjusters, Examiners, and Investigators	$50,660
216.	Electrical and Electronic Engineering Technicians	$50,660
217.	Transportation Inspectors	$50,390
218.	Compensation, Benefits, and Job Analysis Specialists	$50,230
219.	Signal and Track Switch Repairers	$50,150
220.	Anthropologists and Archeologists	$49,930
221.	Criminal Justice and Law Enforcement Teachers, Postsecondary	$49,730
222.	Medical and Clinical Laboratory Technologists	$49,700
223.	Funeral Directors	$49,620
224.	Sales Representatives, Wholesale and Manufacturing, Except Technical and Scientific Products	$49,610
225.	Arbitrators, Mediators, and Conciliators	$49,490

226.	Recreation and Fitness Studies Teachers, Postsecondary	$49,270
227.	Insurance Appraisers, Auto Damage	$49,180
228.	Chemical Plant and System Operators	$49,080
229.	Librarians	$49,080
230.	Subway and Streetcar Operators	$48,980
231.	Railroad Brake, Signal, and Switch Operators	$48,860
232.	Vocational Education Teachers, Secondary School	$48,690
233.	Writers and Authors	$48,640
234.	Historians	$48,520
235.	First-Line Supervisors/Managers of Transportation and Material-Moving Machine and Vehicle Operators	$48,330
236.	Special Education Teachers, Secondary School	$48,330
237.	Surveyors	$48,290
238.	Cartographers and Photogrammetrists	$48,240
239.	Radiologic Technologists and Technicians	$48,170
240.	Sales Representatives, Services, All Other	$48,100
241.	Fire Inspectors and Investigators	$48,050
242.	Training and Development Specialists	$47,830
243.	Animal Scientists	$47,800
244.	Aircraft Mechanics and Service Technicians	$47,740
245.	Secondary School Teachers, Except Special and Vocational Education	$47,740
246.	Special Education Teachers, Middle School	$47,650
247.	Educational, Vocational, and School Counselors	$47,530
248.	Police and Sheriff's Patrol Officers	$47,460
249.	Respiratory Therapists	$47,420
250.	Emergency Management Specialists	$47,410
251.	Public Relations Specialists	$47,350
252.	First-Line Supervisors/Managers of Production and Operating Workers	$47,300
253.	Transit and Railroad Police	$47,080
254.	Compliance Officers, Except Agriculture, Construction, Health and Safety, and Transportation	$47,050
255.	Editors	$46,990
256.	Dieticians and Nutritionists	$46,980
257.	Boilermakers	$46,960
258.	Avionics Technicians	$46,950
259.	Electrical and Electronics Drafters	$46,830
260.	Industrial Engineering Technicians	$46,810
261.	Purchasing Agents and Buyers, Farm Products	$46,770
262.	Broadcast News Analysts	$46,710
263.	Film and Video Editors	$46,670
264.	Construction and Building Inspectors	$46,570
265.	Special Education Teachers, Preschool, Kindergarten, and Elementary School	$46,360

Salary Finder

266.	Curators	$46,300
267.	Middle School Teachers, Except Special and Vocational Education	$46,300
268.	Telecommunications Line Installers and Repairers	$46,280
269.	Plant and System Operators, All Other	$46,270
270.	Precision Instrument and Equipment Repairers, All Other	$46,250
271.	Pile-Driver Operators	$46,180
272.	Geological and Petroleum Technicians	$46,160
273.	Stationary Engineers and Boiler Operators	$46,040
274.	Mechanical Engineering Technicians	$45,850
275.	Millwrights	$45,630
276.	Tax Examiners, Collectors, and Revenue Agents	$45,620
277.	Court Reporters	$45,610
278.	Elementary School Teachers, Except Special Education	$45,570
279.	Control and Valve Installers and Repairers, Except Mechanical Door	$45,440
280.	Aircraft Structure, Surfaces, Rigging, and Systems Assemblers	$45,410
281.	Gas Compressor and Gas Pumping Station Operators	$45,400
282.	Forensic Science Technicians	$45,330
283.	Electrical and Electronics Repairers, Commercial and Industrial Equipment	$45,180
284.	Legal Support Workers, All Other	$45,140
285.	Postal Service Clerks	$44,800
286.	Electro-Mechanical Technicians	$44,720
287.	Wholesale and Retail Buyers, Except Farm Products	$44,640
288.	Appraisers and Assessors of Real Estate	$44,460
289.	Postal Service Mail Carriers	$44,350
290.	Tool and Die Makers	$44,290
291.	Vocational Education Teachers, Middle School	$44,240
292.	Adult Literacy, Remedial Education, and GED Teachers and Instructors	$43,910
293.	Postal Service Mail Sorters, Processors, and Processing Machine Operators	$43,900
294.	Vocational Education Teachers, Postsecondary	$43,900
295.	Designers, All Other	$43,870
296.	Insurance Sales Agents	$43,870
297.	Fish and Game Wardens	$43,700
298.	Mechanical Drafters	$43,700
299.	Electricians	$43,610
300.	Kindergarten Teachers, Except Special Education	$43,580
301.	Social Workers, All Other	$43,580
302.	First-Line Supervisors/Managers of Office and Administrative Support Workers	$43,510
303.	Rail Car Repairers	$43,320
304.	Marriage and Family Therapists	$43,210

305.	Electrical and Electronics Installers and Repairers, Transportation Equipment	$43,110
306.	Property, Real Estate, and Community Association Managers	$43,070
307.	Drafters, All Other	$43,060
308.	Medical and Public Health Social Workers	$43,040
309.	Paralegals and Legal Assistants	$43,040
310.	Food Service Managers	$43,020
311.	Sound Engineering Technicians	$43,010
312.	Brickmasons and Blockmasons	$42,980
313.	Plumbers, Pipefitters, and Steamfitters	$42,770
314.	Advertising Sales Agents	$42,750
315.	Media and Communication Workers, All Other	$42,570
316.	Probation Officers and Correctional Treatment Specialists	$42,500
317.	Numerical Tool and Process Control Programmers	$42,480
318.	Employment, Recruitment, and Placement Specialists	$42,420
319.	Lodging Managers	$42,320
320.	Cardiovascular Technologists and Technicians	$42,300
321.	Interior Designers	$42,260
322.	Therapists, All Other	$42,250
323.	Meeting and Convention Planners	$42,180
324.	Occupational Health and Safety Technicians	$42,160
325.	Occupational Therapist Assistants	$42,060
326.	Model Makers, Metal and Plastic	$42,050
327.	Artists and Related Workers, All Other	$41,990
328.	Fine Artists, Including Painters, Sculptors, and Illustrators	$41,970
329.	Architectural and Civil Drafters	$41,960
330.	Set and Exhibit Designers	$41,820
331.	Farm and Home Management Advisors	$41,710
332.	First-Line Supervisors/Managers, Protective Service Workers, All Other	$41,570
333.	Computer Support Specialists	$41,470
334.	Physical Therapist Assistants	$41,360
335.	Health Educators	$41,330
336.	Locomotive Firers	$41,290
337.	Tapers	$41,280
338.	Roof Bolters, Mining	$41,250
339.	Fire Fighters	$41,190
340.	Gaming Supervisors	$41,160
341.	Athletes and Sports Competitors	$41,060
342.	Industrial Machinery Mechanics	$41,050
343.	Refractory Materials Repairers, Except Brickmasons	$40,780
344.	Archivists	$40,730
345.	Medical Equipment Repairers	$40,580
346.	Civil Engineering Technicians	$40,560
347.	Environmental Engineering Technicians	$40,560
348.	Audio-Visual Collections Specialists	$40,530

349.	Structural Iron and Steel Workers	$40,480
350.	Mobile Heavy Equipment Mechanics, Except Engines	$40,440
351.	Continuous Mining Machine Operators	$40,430
352.	Chemical Equipment Operators and Tenders	$40,290
353.	Camera Operators, Television, Video, and Motion Picture	$40,060
354.	Rail-Track Laying and Maintenance Equipment Operators	$40,000
355.	Mine Cutting and Channeling Machine Operators	$39,990
356.	Graphic Designers	$39,900
357.	Explosives Workers, Ordnance Handling Experts, and Blasters	$39,890
358.	Aircraft Cargo Handling Supervisors	$39,840
359.	Pump Operators, Except Wellhead Pumpers	$39,800
360.	Real Estate Sales Agents	$39,760
361.	Music Directors and Composers	$39,750
362.	Clergy	$39,680
363.	Commercial Divers	$39,590
364.	First-Line Supervisors/Managers of Helpers, Laborers, and Material Movers, Hand	$39,570
365.	Chemical Technicians	$39,240
366.	Riggers	$39,220
367.	Rail Transportation Workers, All Other	$39,150
368.	Respirator Therapy Technicians	$39,120
369.	Shuttle Car Operators	$39,060
370.	Crane and Tower Operators	$39,040
371.	Bridge and Lock Tenders	$39,010
372.	Production, Planning, and Expediting Clerks	$38,620
373.	Rotary Drill Operators, Oil and Gas	$38,460
374.	Reinforcing Iron and Rebar Workers	$38,220
375.	Counselors, All Other	$38,210
376.	Legal Secretaries	$38,190
377.	Tire Builders	$38,120
378.	Agricultural Inspectors	$38,100
379.	Environmental Science and Protection Technicians, Including Health	$39,090
380.	Life, Physical, and Social Science Technicians, All Other	$37,920
381.	Radio Operators	$37,890
382.	Mathematical Technicians	$37,880
383.	Rail Yard Engineers, Dinkey Operators, and Hostlers	$37,880
384.	Embalmers	$37,840
385.	First-Line Supervisors/Managers of Framing, Fishing, and Forestry Workers	$37,750
386.	Education Administrators, Preschool and Child Care Center/Program	$37,740
387.	Radio Mechanics	$37,690
388.	Bus and Truck Mechanics and Diesel Engine Specialists	$37,660
389.	Heating, Air Conditioning, and Refrigeration Mechanics and Installers	$37,660

390.	Airfield Operations Specialists	$37,630
391.	Eligibility Interviewers, Government Programs	$37,540
392.	Child, Family, and School Social Workers	$37,480
393.	Mining Machine Operators, All Other	$37,370
394.	Sheet Metal Workers	$37,360
395.	First-Line Supervisors/Managers of Landscaping, Lawn Service, and Groundskeeping Workers	$37,300
396.	Loading Machine Operators, underground Mining	$37,250
397.	Executive Secretaries and Administrative Assistants	$37,240
398.	Healthcare Practitioners and Technical Workers, All Other	$37,200
399.	Traffic Technicians	$37,140
400.	Framers and Ranchers	$37,130
401.	Cargo and Freight Agents	$37,110
402.	Insulation Workers, Mechanical	$36,900
403.	Operating Engineers and Other Construction Equipment Operators	$36,890
404.	Tile and Marble Setters	$36,590
405.	Athletic Trainers	$36,560
406.	Carpenters	$36,550
407.	Licensed Practical and Licensed Vocational Nurses	$36,480
408.	Computer, Automated Teller, and Office Machine Repairers	$36,480
409.	Brokerage Clerks	$36,390
410.	Law Clerks	$36,360
411.	Derrick Operators, Oil and Gas	$36,240
412.	Wellhead Pumpers	$36,150
413.	Drywall and Ceiling Tile Installers	$36,140
414.	Surgical Technologists	$36,080
415.	Water and Liquid Waste Treatment Plant and System Operators	$36,070
416.	Title Examiners, Abstractors, and Searchers	$36,020
417.	Stonemasons	$35,960
418.	Loan Counselors	$35,790
419.	Correctional Officers and Jailers	$35,760
420.	Biological Technicians	$35,710
421.	Painters, Transportation Equipment	$35,680
422.	Interpreters and Translators	$35,560
423.	Extraction Workers, All Other	$35,450
424.	Hazardous Materials Removal Workers	$35,450
425.	Mental Health and Substance Abuse Social Workers	$35,410
426.	Patternmakers, Metal and Plastic	$35,380
427.	Community and Social Service Specialists, All Other	$35,210
428.	Automotive Body and Related Repairers	$35,180
429.	Health Technologists and Technicians, All Other	$35,140
430.	Truck Drivers, Heavy and Tractors-Trailer	$35,040
431.	Recreational Therapists	$34,990

Salary Finder

432.	Separating, Filtering, Clarifying, Precipitating, and Still Machine Setters, Operators, and Tenders	$34,970
433.	Camera and Photographic Equipment Repairers	$34,850
434.	Audio and Video Equipment Repairers	$34,840
435.	Security and Fire Alarm Systems Installers	$34,810
436.	Machinists	$34,770
437.	Metal Workers and Plastic Workers, All Other	$34,710
438.	Plasterers and Stucco Masons	$34,700
439.	Choreographers	$34,660
440.	Glaziers	$34,610
441.	Carpet Installers	$34,560
442.	Maintenance Workers, Machinery	$34,550
443.	Earth Drillers, Except Oil and Gas	$34,500
444.	Mental Health Counselors	$34,380
445.	Chefs and Head Cooks	$34,370
446.	Museum Technicians and Conservators	$34,340
447.	Directors, Religious Activities and Education	$34,260
448.	Sales and Related Workers, All Other	$34,250
449.	Bailiffs	$34,210
450.	Floor Layers, Except Carpet, Wood and Hard Tiles	$34,190
451.	Telephone Operators	$34,140
452.	Desktop Publishers	$34,130
453.	Substance Abuse and Behavioral Disorder Counselors	$34,040
454.	First-Line Supervisors/Managers of Retail Sales Workers	$33,960
455.	Home Appliance Repairers	$33,860
456.	Social Science Research Assistants	$33,860
457.	Dredge Operators	$33,820
458.	Automotive Service Technicians and Mechanics	$33,780
459.	Human Resources Assistants, Except Payroll and Timekeeping	$33,750
460.	Private Detectives and Investigators	$33,750
461.	Paperhangers	$33,710
462.	Hoist and Winch Operators	$33,620
463.	Lay-Out Workers, Metal and Plastic	$33,600
464.	Computer Operators	$33,560
465.	Reporters and Correspondents	$33,470
466.	Self-Enrichment Education Teachers	$33,440
467.	Massage Therapists	$33,400
468.	Survey Researchers	$33,360
469.	Prepress Technicians and Workers	$33,310
470.	Engine and Other Machine Assemblers	$33,250
471.	Motorboat Mechanics	$33,210
472.	Procurement Clerks	$33,100
473.	Forest Fire Inspectors and Prevention Specialists	$32,940
474.	Installation, Maintenance, and Repair Workers, All Other	$32,940

475. Excavating and Loading Machine and Dragline
     Operators $32,930
476. Service Unit Operators, Oil, Gas and Mining $32,910
477. Electric Motor, Power Tool, and Related Repairers $32,860
478. Semiconductor Processors $32,860
479. Medical and Clinical Laboratory Technicians $32,840
480. First-Line Supervisors/Managers of Personal Service
     Workers $32,800
481. Fabric and Apparel Patternmakers $32,730
482. Cement Masons and Concrete Finishers $32,650
483. Metal-Refining Furnace Operators and Tenders $32,650
484. Dental Laboratory Technicians $32,580
485. Job Printers $32,410
486. Payroll and Timekeeping Clerks $32,400
487. Motorboat Operators $32,350
488. Surveying and Mapping Technicians $32,340
489. Roofers $32,260
490. Dispatchers, Except Police, Fire and Ambulance $32,190
491. Education, Training, and Library Workers, All Other $32,160
492. Lathe and Turning Machine Tool Setters, Operators,
     and Tenders, Metal and Plastic $32,160
493. Bus Drivers, Transit and Intercity $32,090
494. Locksmiths and Safe Repairers $32,020
495. Tank Car, Truck, and Ship Loaders $31,970
496. Maintenance and Repair Workers, General $31,910
497. Logging Workers, All Other $31,870
498. Makeup Artists, Theatrical and Performance $31,820
499. Agricultural and Food Science Technicians $31,730
500. Communications Equipment Operators, All Other $31,680
501. Computer-Controlled Machine Tool Operators, Metal
     and Plastic $31,670
502. Terrazzo Workers and Finishers $31,630
503. Mechanical Door Repairers $31,610
504. Milling and Planing Machine Setters, Operators, and
     Tenders, Metal and Plastic $31,570
505. Highway Maintenance Workers $31,540
506. Patternmakers, Wood $31,510
507. Recreational Vehicle Service Technicians $31,510
508. Paper Goods Machine Setters, Operators, and Tenders $31,490
509. Police, Fire, and Ambulance Dispatchers $31,470
510. Septic Tank Servicers and Sewer Pipe Cleaners $31,430
511. Welders, Cutters, Solderers, and Brazers $31,400
512. Paving, Surfacing, and Tamping Equipment Operators $31,300
513. First-Line Supervisors/Managers of Housekeeping and
     Janitorial Workers $31,290
514. Statistical Assistants $31,250
515. Painters, Construction and Maintenance $31,190

516.	Medical Appliance Technicians	$31,180
517.	Information and Record Clerks, All Other	$31,150
518.	Insurance Claims and Policy Processing Clerks	$31,120
519.	Rolling Machine Setters, Operators, and Tenders, Metal and Plastic	$31,050
520.	Printing Machine Operators	$30,990
521.	Court, Municipal, and License Clerks	$30,980
522.	Welding, Soldering, and Brazing Machine Setters, Operators, and Tenders	$30,980
523.	Loan Interviewers and Clerks	$30,970
524.	Watch Repairers	$30,900
525.	Forest and Conservation Technicians	$30,880
526.	Heat Treating Equipment Setters, Operators, and Tenders, Metal and Plastic	$30,850
527.	Automotive Glass Installers and Repairers	$30,720
528.	Broadcast Technicians	$30,690
529.	Tool Grinders, Filers, and Sharpeners	$30,640
530.	Sailors and Marine Oilers	$30,630
531.	Bookkeeping, Accounting, and Auditing Clerks	$30,560
532.	Multiple Machine Tool Setters, Operators, and Tenders, Metal and Plastic	$30,530
533.	Insulation Workers, Floor Ceiling, and Wall	$30,510
534.	Construction and Related Workers, All Other	$30,470
535.	Meter Readers, Utilities	$30,330
536.	Pipelayers	$30,330
537.	Furnace, Kiln, Oven, Drier, and Kettle Operators and Tenders	$30,320
538.	Opticians, Dispensing	$30,300
539.	Structural Metal Fabricators and Fitters	$30,290
540.	Material Moving Workers, All Others	$30,270
541.	Bookbinders	$30,260
542.	Dental Assistants	$30,220
543.	Transportation Workers, All Other	$30,180
544.	Parking Enforcement Workers	$30,160
545.	Motorcycle Mechanics	$30,050
546.	Electronic Home Entertainment Equipment Installers and Repairers	$29,980
547.	Credit Authorizers, Checkers, and Clerks	$29,970
548.	Medical Transcriptionists	$29,950
549.	Drilling and Boring Machine Tool Setters, Operators, and Tenders, Metal and Plastic	$29,870
550.	Jewelers and Precious Stone and Metal Workers	$29,750
551.	Logging Equipment Operators	$29,700
552.	Pourers and Casters, Metal	$29,570
553.	Farm Equipment Mechanics	$29,460
554.	Word Processors and Typists	$29,430
555.	Inspectors, Testers, Sorters, Samplers, and Weighers	$29,420

556.	Mixing and Blending Machine Setters, Operators, and Tenders	$29,330
557.	Log Graders and Scalers	$29,240
558.	Travel Agents	$29,210
559.	Musical Instrument Repairers and Tuners	$29,200
560.	Rehabilitation Counselors	$29,200
561.	Bill and Account Collectors	$29,050
562.	Forging Machine Setters, Operators, and Tenders, Metal and Plastic	$28,980
563.	Refuse and Recyclable Material Collectors	$28,970
564.	Floor Sanders and Finishers	$28,890
565.	Billing and Posting Clerks and Machine Operators	$28,850
566.	Timing Device Assemblers, Adjusters, and Calibrators	$28,830
567.	Foundry Mold and Coremakers	$28,740
568.	Coin, Vending, and Amusement Machine Servicers and Repairers	$28,710
569.	Fallers	$28,710
570.	Correspondence Clerks	$28,700
571.	Segmental Pavers	$28,700
572.	Helpers-Extraction Workers	$28,680
573.	Extruding and Forming Machine Setters, Operators, and Tenders, Synthetic and Glass Fibers	$28,670
574.	Teachers and Instructors, All Other	$28,660
575.	Reservation and Transportation Ticket Agents and Travel Clerks	$28,540
576.	Model Makers, Wood	$28,470
577.	Travel Guides	$28,460
578.	New Accounts, Clerks	$28,390
579.	Fabric Menders, Except Garment	$28,370
580.	Customer Service Representatives	$28,330
581.	Extruding and Drawing Machine Setters, Operators, and Tenders, Metal and Plastic	$28,250
582.	Tree Trimmers and Pruners	$28,250
583.	Electronic Equipment Installers and Repairers, Motor Vehicles	$28,220
584.	Medical Secretaries	$28,090
585.	Crushing, Grinding, and Polishing Machine Setters, Operators, and Tenders	$28,080
586.	Grinding, Lapping, Polishing, and Buffing Machine Tool Setters, Operators, and Tenders, Metal and Plastic	$28,080
587.	Medical Records and Health Information Technicians	$28,030
588.	Cutting and Slicing Machine Setters, Operators, and Tenders	$27,930
589.	Animal Control Workers	$27,910
590.	Pest Control Workers	$27,880
591.	Graduate Teaching Assistants	$27,840
592.	Psychiatric Technicians	$27,780

Salary Finder 173

593.	Extruding, Forming, Pressing, and Compacting Machine Setters, Operators, and Tenders, Metal and Plastic	$27,710
594.	Electromechanical Equipment Assemblers	$27,560
595.	Plating and Coating Machine Setters, Operators, and Tenders, Metal and Plastic	$27,470
596.	Proofreaders and Copy Markers	$27,450
597.	Secretaries, Except Legal, Medical, and Executive	$27,450
598.	Parts Salespersons	$27,430
599.	Tax Preparers	$27,360
600.	Industrial Truck and Tractor Operators	$27,270
601.	Fishers and Related Fishing Workers	$27,250
602.	Upholsterers	$27,230
603.	Conveyor Operators and Tenders	$27,220
604.	Office and Administrative Support Workers, All Other	$27,200
605.	Gaming Surveillance Officers and Gaming Investigators	$27,130
606.	Rock Splitters, Quarry	$27,130
607.	Animal Breeders	$27,090
608.	Emergency Medical Technicians and Paramedics	$27,070
609.	Cabinetmakers and Bench Carpenters	$27,010
610.	Healthcare Support Workers, All Other	$26,990
611.	First-Line Supervisors/Managers of Food Preparation and Serving Workers	$26,980
612.	Coaches and Scouts	$26,950
613.	Butchers and Meat Cutters	$26,930
614.	Protective Service Workers, All Other	$26,920
615.	Outdoor Power Equipment and Other Small Engine Mechanics	$26,910
616.	Coating, Painting, and Spraying Machine Setters, Operators, and Tenders	$26,830
617.	Veterinary Technologists and Technicians	$26,780
618.	Assemblers and Fabricators, All Other	$26,730
619.	Pesticide Handlers, Sprayers, and Applicators, Vegetation	$26,700
620.	Library Technicians	$26,560
621.	Fence Erectors	$26,400
622.	Cutting, Punching, and Press Machine Setters, Operators, and Tenders, Metal and Plastic	$26,340
623.	Order Clerks	$26,340
624.	Construction Laborers	$26,320
625.	Animal Trainers	$26,310
626.	Coil Winders, Tapers, and Finishers	$26,300
627.	Interviews, Except Eligibility and Loan	$26,290
628.	Medical Assistants	$26,290
629.	Photographers	$26,170
630.	Skin Care Specialists	$26,170
631.	Shipping, Receiving, and Traffic Clerks	$26,070
632.	Fiberglass Laminators and Fabricators	$25,980
633.	Medical Equipment Preparers	$25,950

634.	Fitness Trainers and Aerobics Instructors	$25,910
635.	Costume Attendants	$25,740
636.	Roustabouts, Oil and Gas	$25,700
637.	Pharmacy Technicians	$25,630
638.	Etchers and Engravers	$25,590
639.	Social and Human Service Assistants	$25,580
640.	Bindery Workers	$25,570
641.	Electrical and Electronic Equipment Assemblers	$25,560
642.	Molding, Coremaking, and Casting Machine Setters, Operators, and Tenders, Metal and Plastic	$25,560
643.	Ophthalmic Laboratory Technicians	$25,460
644.	Weighers, Measurers, Checkers, and Samplers, Recordkeeping	$25,370
645.	Helpers - Brickmasons, Blockmasons, Stonemasons, and Tile and Marble Setters	$25,350
646.	Truck Drivers, Light or Delivery Services	$25,300
647.	Cementing and Gluing Machine Operators and Tenders	$25,170
648.	Building Cleaning Workers, All Other	$25,090
649.	Manufactured Building and Mobile Home Installers	$25,080
650.	Occupational Therapist Aides	$25,020
651.	Furniture Finishers	$25,010
652.	Molders, Shapers, and Casters, Except Metal and Plastic	$25,010
653.	Public Address System and Other Announcers	$24,990
654.	Production Workers, All Other	$24,890
655.	Bus Drivers, School	$24,820
656.	Data Entry Keyers	$24,690
657.	Concierges	$24,600
658.	Office Machine Operators, Except Computer	$24,540
659.	Religious Workers, All Other	$24,330
660.	Radio and Television Announcers	$24,310
661.	Textile Knitting and Weaving Machine Setters, Operators and Tenders	$24,290
662.	Sawing Machine Setters, Operators, and Tenders, Wood	$24,280
663.	Team Assemblers	$24,190
664.	Craft Artists	$24,090
665.	Dietetic Technicians	$24,040
666.	Woodworking Machine Setters, Operators, and Tenders, Except Sawing	$23,940
667.	Helpers - Pipelayers, Plumbers, Pipefitters, and Steamfitters	$23,910
668.	Psychiatric Aides	$23,900
669.	Cooling and Freezing Equipment Operators and Tenders	$23,880
670.	Grinding and Polishing Workers, Hand	$23,880
671.	Merchandise Displayers and Window Trimmers	$23,820
672.	Mail Clerks and Mail Machine Operators, Except Postal Service	$23,810
673.	Helpers - Electricians	$23,760

Salary Finder

674.	Office Clerks, General	$23,710
675.	Farm Labor Contractors	$23,550
676.	Food and Tobacco Roasting, Baking, and Drying Machine Operators and Tenders	$23,510
677.	Models	$23,340
678.	Textile Bleaching and Dyeing Machine Operators and Tenders	$23,290
679.	Photographic Process Workers	$23,280
680.	Barbers	$23,150
681.	Gaming Cage Workers	$23,150
682.	Food Batchmakers	$23,100
683.	Helpers - Carpenters	$23,060
684.	Textile Winding, Twisting, and Drawing Out Machine Setters, Operators, and Tenders	$23,050
685.	Packaging and Filling Machine Operators and Tenders	$22,990
686.	Painting, Coating and Decorating Workers	$22,970
687.	Textile, Apparel, and Furnishing Workers, All Other	$22,950
688.	Tailors, Dressmakers, and Custom Sewers	$22,910
689.	Receptionists and Information Clerks	$22,900
690.	Umpires, Referees, and Other Sports Officials	$22,880
691.	Cooks, Private Household	$22,870
692.	Cleaning, Washing, and Metal Pickling Equipment Operators and Tenders	$22,850
693.	Helpers, Construction Trades, All Other	$22,760
694.	Slot Key Persons	$22,720
695.	Motor Vehicle Operators, All Other	$22,710
696.	Preschool Teachers, Except Special Education	$22,680
697.	Residential Advisors	$22,670
698.	Machine Feeders and Offbearers	$22,640
699.	Switchboard Operators, Including Answering Service	$22,640
700.	Woodworkers, All Other	$22,580
701.	Agricultural Workers, All Other	$22,470
702.	Cutters and Trimmers, Hand	$22,330
703.	Helpers - Installation, Maintenance, and Repair Workers	$22,270
704.	Nursing Aides, Orderlies, and Attendants	$22,180
705.	Demonstrators and Product Promoters	$22,150
706.	Tellers	$22,140
707.	File Clerks	$22,090
708.	Physical Therapist Aides	$22,060
709.	Bakers	$22,030
710.	Shoe Machine Operators and Tenders	$21,910
711.	Gaming Service Workers, All Other	$21,890
712.	Bicycle Repairers	$21,790
713.	Helpers - Roofers	$21,760
714.	Floral Designers	$21,700
715.	Slaughterers and Meat Packers	$21,690
716.	Library Assistants, Clerical	$21,640

717.	Textile Cutting Machine Setters, Operators, and Tenders	$21,620
718.	Cooks, All Other	$21,610
719.	Couriers and Messengers	$21,540
720.	Security Guards	$21,530
721.	Tire Repairers and Changers	$21,340
722.	Helpers - Painters, Paperhangers, Plasters, and Stucco Masons	$21,330
723.	Hairdressers, Hairstylists, and Cosmetologists	$21,320
724.	Food Cooking Machine Operators and Tenders	$21,280
725.	Landscaping and Groundskeeping Workers	$21,260
726.	Laborers and Freight, Stock and Material Movers, Hand	$21,220
727.	Crossing Guards	$21,060
728.	Telemarketers	$20,990
729.	Forest and Conservation Workers	$20,810
730.	Driver/Sales Workers	$20,770
731.	Helpers - Production Workers	$20,740
732.	Teacher Assistants	$20,740
733.	Gaming Change Persons and Booth Cashiers	$20,680
734.	Recreation Workers	$20,470
735.	Shoe and Leather Workers and Repairers	$20,450
736.	Stock Clerks and Order Fillers	$20,440
737.	Grounds Maintenance Workers, All Other	$20,420
738.	Tour Guides and Escorts	$20,420
739.	Cooks, Institution and Cafeteria	$20,410
740.	Ambulance Drivers and Attendants, Except Emergency Medical Technicians	$20,370
741.	Meat, Poultry, and Fish Cutters and Trimmers	$20,370
742.	Sewers, Hand	$20,370
743.	Funeral Attendants	$20,350
744.	Taxi Driers and Chauffeurs	$20,350
745.	Cooks, Restaurant	$20,340
746.	Agricultural Equipment Operators	$20,230
747.	Door-To-Door Sales Workers, News and Street Vendors, and Related Workers	$20,190
748.	Transportation Attendants, Except Flight Attendants and Baggage Porters	$20,070
749.	Veterinary Assistants and Laboratory Animal Caretakers	$19,960
750.	Janitors and Cleaners, Except Maids and Housekeeping Cleaners	$19,930
751.	Retail Salespersons	$19,760
752.	Counter and Rental Clerks	$19,570
753.	Photographic Processing Machine Operators	$19,500
754.	Pharmacy Aides	$19,440
755.	Home Health Aides	$19,420
756.	Manicurists and Pedicurists	$19,190
757.	Farmworkers, Farm and Ranch Animals	$19,060
758.	Personal Care and Service Workers, All Other	$18,970

759.	Sewing Machine Operators	$18,810
760.	Gaming and Sports Book Writers and Runners	$18,800
761.	Locker Room, Coatroom, and Dressing Room Attendants	$18,610
762.	Hotel, Motel, and Resort Desk Clerks	$18,460
763.	Baggage Porters and Bellhops	$18,360
764.	Nonfarm Animal Caretakers	$18,140
765.	Food Servers, Nonrestaurant	$18,090
766.	Cleaners of Vehicles and Equipment	$18,060
767.	Cooks, Short Order	$17,880
768.	Laundry and Dry-Cleaning Workers	$17,850
769.	Pressers, Textile, Garment, and Related Materials	$17,800
770.	Food Preparation and Serving Related Workers, All Other	$17,780
771.	Personal and Home Care Aides	$17,770
772.	Service Station Attendants	$17,750
773.	Packers and Packagers, Hand	$17,650
774.	Child Care Workers	$17,630
775.	Maids and Housekeeping Cleaners	$17,580
776.	Motion Picture Projectionists	$17,450
777.	Food Preparation Workers	$17,410
778.	Parking Lot Attendants	$17,320
779.	Graders and Sorters, Agricultural Products	$17,200
780.	Lifeguards, Ski Patrol, and Other Recreational Protective Service Workers	$17,160
781.	Cashiers	$16,810
782.	Farmworkers and Laborers, Crop, Nursery, and Greenhouse	$16,540
783.	Bartenders	$16,350
784.	Amusement and Recreation Attendants	$16,290
785.	Hosts and Hostesses, Restaurant, Lounge, and Coffee Shop	$16,170
786.	Shampooers	$16,170
787.	Counter Attendants, Cafeteria, Food Concession, and Coffee Shop	$16,130
788.	Ushers, Lobby Attendants, and Ticket Takers	$15,880
789.	Dishwashers	$15,750
790.	Legislators	$15,660
791.	Cooks, Fast Food	$15,410
792.	Dining Room and Cafeteria Attendants and Bartender Helpers	$15,310
793.	Combined Food Preparation and Service Workers, Including Fast Food	$15,050
794.	Waiters and Waitresses	$14,850
795.	Gaming Dealers	$14,730

Again, use this information as a reference point for conducting your own salary survey. You will discover that salaries in your particular state and community will differ from the salaries we have identified for the nation as a whole.

12

Continuing Salary Success

IF YOU WANT TO CONTINUE making what you're really worth, you need to make a habit of periodically negotiating compensation. Whatever you do, make sure you combine your qualifications and salary negotiation skills with a knowledge of salaries and salary ranges. When you talk about compensation, which ideally should occur **after** you've received a job offer or during an annual performance appraisal tied to a salary review, do so from a position of strength.

Always communicate your value to employers based upon an understanding of your relevant skills and accomplishments. As an employer- rather than self-centered individual, you want to tell employers what you will do for them rather than what you want them to do for you.

The skills, strategies, techniques, and resources outlined throughout this book should prepare you well for the critical salary negotiation session with employers. Indeed, if you engage in the data gathering and skill building activities we've suggested, you should be well prepared to achieve salary success during the job search as well as on the job. The result should be thousands of dollars in additional income for you over the coming years.

Better still, when you clearly communicate your qualifications and value to employers, they will assign higher value to you than to other individuals who are less oriented toward translating their performance into higher salaries. You'll be a much smarter, and hopefully more richly rewarded, job seeker or employee if you do. Best of all, you'll know what you're worth, and you'll get it!

Index

A
Abbott, Langer, and Associates, 57
Accomplishments, 114, 149
Achievements, 66
Administration, 51, 148
Ads, 83-95
Agreements, 142-143
Applications, 24, 83
Associations, 57-58, 63
Attitude, 71, 81, 143
Audience, 114

B
Benefits:
    calculating, 6, 24-25
    emphasizing, 31
    flexible, 130
    job, 24-25
    negotiating, 131-138
    non-negotiable, 131
    options, 130-132
    retirement, 131
    trends in, 34-36
Businesses:
    small, 45
    starting, 45

C
Cafeteria plans, 43-44
Capabilities, 54
Child care, 42-43
Class, 77
Classified ads, 53, 59-60
Close, 143-144
Collective bargaining, 41
Common ground, 79
Communication, 12, 101
Compensation: 15, 19
    calculating, 6-8
    elements, 6-8
    executive-level, 46
    flexible, 37
    language of, 1
    options, 46-47
    package, 6, 25-26, 33
    questions, 83
    total, 25
    trends, 33-47
    under-, 5, 10
Competence, 73
Content, 114-117
Contingency workers, 45
Cost containment, 36, 43
Cost-of-living increases, 38, 54, 148

D
Diary, 149
Diction, 112
Dishonesty, 32
Duties, 140

E
Eldercare, 42-43
Employers:
  expectations of, 55
  focusing on, 100
  time, 76-77
  valuing of, 49
Equity:
  incentives, 27, 132
  principles of, 148
Examples, 76
Executive search firms, 57

F
Feedback, 101
Fillers, 113
Flexibility, 46-47
Follow through, 143-144
Follow-up, 31

G
Give backs, 38
Goals, 72
Going rates, 20, 49-55
Grammar, 112

H
Happiness, 28-29, 32
Hobbies, 114-115
Honesty, 32, 71

I
Image, 31
Insurance:
  disability, 41
  health, 41
  life, 41
Interview:
  conducting, 96-120
  controlling, 119
  principles, 97-102
  questions, 97
Interviewers, 102

J
Job:
  enjoying, 19-20
  hedgers, 133
  hopping, 133
  interviews, 96-120
  listings, 59-60
  lock, 133
  offer, 23-24, 83, 139-145
  value of, 34

L
Language, 116
Leave, 44
Letters:
  acceptance, 145
  thank-you, 81, 144
Library, 65-66
Listeners, 73, 114
Listening, 99-100
Luck, 74
Lying, 32, 89

M
Memorizing, 79
Myths, 16-29, 146-148

N
National Association of Colleges and Employers, 58
Negatives:
  discussing, 98-99
  overcoming, 117-119
  using, 133
Negotiating:
  environments, 18
  leverage, 21
  techniques, 122-127
  willingness, 17-18, 124
Networking, 60-62, 64, 73-74
Networks, 150
Newspapers, 59
Nonverbal, 101
Note taking, 79

O
Objections, 117-119, 127-130
Offers:
  accepting, 143-144
  considering, 140-141
  receiving, 23
  written, 142-143
Outcomes, 150

Index

P
Parental leave, 42-43
Performance:
  appraisals, 22, 147
  communicating, 141
  compensation for, 20
  documenting, 65-67, 149
  job, 22
  myth of, 146-148
Perks, 6
Planning, 72
Positions:
  changing, 19
  creating, 136
  entry-level, 18, 49
  higher-level, 18, 40
Positive:
  content, 114-117
  form, 112-113
Power:
  bargaining, 39
  feelings of, 9
  sucking up to, 147
  talking money to, 1-2
Preparation, 69

Q
Qualifications, 30, 136
Questions:
  answering, 78, 100-101, 105-110
  asking, 72, 78, 102-105, 110-112
  neutralizing, 103

R
Raises, 146-152
Realism, 79-80
Reimbursement accounts, 43
Renegotiations, 134-135
Resources, 14, 81-82
Respect, 80
Responsibilities, 140
Retirement, 40-41, 44
Robert Half International, 57
Rules, 70-82

S
Salary:
  acceptance, 26-27
  adequate, 46
  approach, 13-14
  calculating, 49-55, 89
  caps, 38
  clues, 86
  comparative, 50, 55-62
  cues, 8
  determiners, 6, 17, 28
  discussing, 23
  equitable, 50
  expectations, 6
  flexibility, 122-124
  going rate for, 49-53
  government, 9
  gross, 25
  history, 88-92
  increases, 146-153
  increments, 10
  information, 13, 53, 87-88
  initiative, 151
  I.Q., 2-5
  issues, 83
  mistakes, 29-32
  myths, 16-29
  negotiations, 18
  non-negotiable, 18, 51-52
  norm, 51
  objections, 127-130
  personalizing, 30
  positions, 49
  questions, 33, 102-105, 121
  ranges, 10, 17, 49, 93-95, 126-127
  realities, 16-29
  requirements, 24, 29, 92-93, 125
  resources, 14
  review, 146
  schedules, 51
  secrecy, 8, 50
  skills, 2-5, 9, 13-14
  smarts, 2-5, 7-8, 11-12
  starting, 42
  structure, 49-50
  studies, 55-56
  surveys, 9, 53, 62
  talking about, 8
  threats, 21, 152
  winning, 12
Sales, 19

Secrecy, 8, 9, 51
Small businesses, 45
Social security, 35
Stock options, 27, 132-134
Strengths, 98
Success, 70-82
Summarizing, 105-107
Supervisors, 28
Supplemental pay, 44
Supports, 30, 31, 76, 101

T
Tact, 73
Talent, 52, 133
Talking, 5, 8
Teachers, 10
Telephone, 84
Terminology:
 indecisive, 113
 negative, 113, 115
Thoughtfulness, 81
Threats, 21, 152-153
Time, 77, 139
Timing, 31

U
Unions, 41, 137

V
Vacancy announcements (see Ads)
Value:
 assigning, 65
 calculating, 67-68
 communicating, 12
 determining, 85
 documenting, 75-76
 giving, 15
 individuals, 48-49, 52
 positions, 48-49
 stressing, 91
 yourself, 75
Verbs, 113
Visibility, 150
Vision, 1
Vocalized pauses, 113

W
Websites, 63-64
Worth:
 calculating, 5-6
 knowing your, 2, 9, 48
 over-value, 30
 salary reflecting, 20
 under-value, 30
 your, 48

The Authors

FOR MORE THAN TWO DECADES Ron and Caryl Krannich have pursued a passion – assisting hundreds of thousands of individuals, from students, the unemployed, and ex-offenders to military personnel, international job seekers, and CEOs, in making critical job and career transitions. Focusing on key job search skills, career changes, and employment fields, their impressive body of work has helped shape career thinking and behavior both in the United States and abroad. Their sound advice has changed numerous lives, including their own!

Ron and Caryl are two of America's leading career and travel writers who have authored more than 80 books. A former Peace Corps Volunteer and Fulbright Scholar, Ron received his Ph.D. in Political Science from Northern Illinois University. Caryl received her Ph.D. in Speech Communication from Penn State University. Together they operate Development Concepts Incorporated, a training, consulting, and publishing firm in Virginia.

The Krannichs are both former university professors, high school teachers, management trainers, and consultants. As trainers and consultants, they have completed numerous projects on management, career development, local government, population planning, and rural development in the United States and abroad. Their career books focus on key job search skills, military and civilian career transitions, government and international careers, ex-offenders and re-entry, travel jobs, and nonprofit organizations. and include such bestselling classics as *High Impact Resumes and Letters*, *Interview for Success*, and *Change Your Job, Change Your Life*, which continue in print after more than 20 years.

The Krannichs' books represent one of today's most comprehensive collections of career writing. With over 3 million copies in print, their publications are widely available in bookstores, libraries, and career centers. No strangers to the world of Internet employment and travel, they have written *America's Top Internet Job Sites*, *Haldane's Best Employment Websites for Professionals*, *The Directory of Websites for International Jobs*, and *Travel Planning on the Internet*, and published several Internet recruitment and job search books. Ron served as the first Work Abroad Advisor to Monster.com. Ron and Caryl also have developed three career-related websites: www.impactpublications.com, www.exoffenderreentry.com, and www.veteransworld.com. Many of their career tips appear on such popular websites as www.monster.com, www.careerbuilder.com, www.campuscareercenter.com, and www.employmentguide.com.

Ron and Caryl live a double life with travel being their best kept *"do what you love"* career secret. Authors of more than 20 travel-shopping guidebooks on various destinations around the world, they continue to pursue their international and travel interests through their innovative *Treasures and Pleasures of . . . Best of the Best* travel-shopping series and related website: www.ishoparoundtheworld.com. When not found at their home and business in Virginia, they are probably somewhere in Europe, Asia, Africa, the Middle East, the South Pacific, the Caribbean, or the Americas following their other passion – researching and writing about quality antiques, arts, crafts, jewelry, hotels, restaurants, and sightseeing as well as adhering to the career advice they give to others: *"Pursue a passion that enables you to do what you really love to do."* Their passion is best represented on www.ishoparoundtheworld.com.

As both career and travel experts, the Krannichs' work is frequently featured in major newspapers, magazines, and newsletters as well as on radio, television, and the Internet. Available for interviews, consultation, and presentations, they can be contacted as follows:

krannich@impactpublications.com

Career Resources

THE FOLLOWING CAREER resources are available directly from Impact Publications. Full descriptions of each title as well as downloadable catalogs, videos, software, games, posters, and related products can be found at www.impactpublications.com. Career books by the authors (35) are highlighted in **bold** on pages 187-193. Complete this form or list the titles, include shipping (see formula at the end), enclose payment, and send your order to:

IMPACT PUBLICATIONS
9104 Manassas Drive, Suite N
Manassas Park, VA 20111-5211 USA
1-800-361-1055 (orders only)
Tel. 703-361-7300 or Fax 703-335-9486
E-mail address: query@impactpublications.com
Quick & easy online ordering: www.impactpublications.com

Orders from individuals must be prepaid by check, money order, or major credit card. We accept telephone, fax, and e-mail orders.

Qty.	TITLES	Price	TOTAL

Featured Title

| | Give Me More Money! | $17.95 | |

Salary Negotiations and Surveys

	101 Salary Secrets	12.95	
	250 Best-Paying Jobs	16.95	
	American Salaries and Wages Survey	251.00	
	Get a Raise in 7 Days	14.95	
	Get More Money on Your Next Job	14.95	
	Negotiating Your Salary	14.95	

____	Next-Day Salary Negotiation	8.95 ____
____	Perfect Phrases for Negotiating Salary and Job Offers	9.95 ____
____	Salary Facts Handbook	39.95 ____
____	**Salary Negotiation Tips for Professionals**	16.95 ____
____	Secrets of Power Salary Negotiating	13.99 ____
____	Sweaty Palms	13.95 ____

Interviews

____	101 Dynamite Questions to Ask At Your Job Interview	13.95 ____
____	301 Smart Answers to Tough Interview Questions	10.95 ____
____	501+ Great Interview Questions for Employers and the Best Answers for Prospective Employers	24.95 ____
____	Adams Job Interview Almanac	17.95 ____
____	The Best Answer	13.00 ____
____	Best Answers to 202 Job Interview Questions	17.95 ____
____	Don't Blow the Interview	12.95 ____
____	Everything Practice Interview Book	12.95 ____
____	High-Impact Interview Questions	17.95 ____
____	How to Ace the Brain Teaser Interview	14.95 ____
____	**I Can't Believe They Asked Me That!**	17.95 ____
____	Interview Magic	16.95 ____
____	**Job Interview Tips for People With Not-So-Hot Backgrounds**	14.95 ____
____	Job Interviews for Dummies	16.99 ____
____	Job Interviews That Get You Hired	12.95 ____
____	KeyWords to Nail Your Job Interview	17.95 ____
____	Mastering the Job Interview and Winning the Money Game	12.95 ____
____	Monster Careers: Interviewing	15.00 ____
____	**Nail the Job Interview!**	14.95 ____
____	Perfect Phrases for the Perfect Interview	9.95 ____
____	Pocket Idiot's Guide to Interview Questions and Answers	9.95 ____
____	The Savvy Interviewer	10.95 ____
____	**Win the Interview, Win the Job**	15.95 ____
____	Winning the Interview Game	12.95 ____
____	Winning Job Interviews	12.99 ____
____	Winning the Interview Game	12.95 ____
____	You Have 3 Minutes!	21.95 ____
____	You Got the Interview: Now What?	12.95 ____
____	**You Should Hire Me!**	15.95 ____

Key Directories

____	Associations USA	95.00 ____
____	Encyclopedia of Associations	750.00 ____
____	Encyclopedia of Careers and Vocational Guidance	295.00 ____
____	Enhanced Occupational Outlook Handbook	39.95/49.95 ____
____	Ferguson Career Resource Guide for Women and Minorities	125.00 ____
____	Ferguson Career Resource Guide for Apprenticeship Programs	125.00 ____

Career Resources

____	Ferguson Career Resource Guide for Women and Minorities	125.00 ____
____	Ferguson Career Resource Guide to Internships and Summer Jobs	125.00 ____
____	Headquarters USA	216.00 ____
____	Job Hunter's Sourcebook	175.00 ____
____	New Guide for Occupational Exploration	39.95/49.95 ____
____	Occupational Outlook Handbook	19.95/25.95 ____
____	O*NET Dictionary of Occupational Titles	39.95/49.95 ____

Attitude and Motivation

____	100 Ways to Motivate Yourself	14.99 ____
____	Attitude Is Everything	14.95 ____
____	Change Your Attitude	15.99 ____
____	Change Your Thinking, Change Your Life	18.95 ____
____	Eat That Frog!	15.95 ____
____	Flight Plan	19.95 ____
____	Goals!	15.95 ____
____	Little Gold Book of YES! Attitude	19.99 ____
____	Reinventing Yourself	18.99 ____
____	The Secret	23.95 ____
____	Success Principles	15.95 ____

Inspiration and Empowerment

____	7 Habits of Highly Effective People	15.95 ____
____	The 8th Habit	15.00 ____
____	**101 Secrets of Highly Effective Speakers**	**15.95** ____
____	Create Your Own Future	24.95 ____
____	The Habit Change Workbook	19.95 ____
____	Life Strategies	13.95 ____
____	The Magic of Thinking Big	14.00 ____
____	The Power of Positive Thinking	14.00 ____
____	Power of Purpose	20.00 ____
____	Self Matters	14.00 ____
____	The Story of You	19.99 ____
____	Think Big	12.99 ____
____	Who Moved My Cheese?	19.95 ____

Testing and Assessment

____	Career, Aptitude, and Selections Tests	17.95 ____
____	Career Match	15.00 ____
____	Career Tests	12.95 ____
____	Discover What You're Best At	14.00 ____
____	Do What You Are	18.99 ____
____	Employment Personality Tests Decoded	16.99 ____
____	The Everything Career Tests Book	12.95 ____
____	Finding Your Perfect Work	16.95 ____
____	Go Put Your Strengths to Work	30.00 ____
____	I Could Do Anything If Only I Knew What It Was	16.00 ____

____ I Want to Do Something Else, But I'm Not Sure What It Is	15.95	____
____ Now, Discover Your Strengths	30.00	____
____ Pathfinder	16.00	____
____ Smarts: Are You Hardwired for Success?	21.95	____
____ StrengthsFinder 2.0	19.95	____
____ What Should I Do With My Life?	14.95	____
____ What Type Am I?	14.95	____
____ What's Your Type of Career?	18.95	____
____ Who Do You Think You Are?	18.00	____

Career Exploration and Job Strategies

____ 25 Jobs That Have It All	14.95	____
____ 40 Best Fields for Your Career	16.95	____
____ 50 Best Jobs for Your Personality	16.95	____
____ 50 Cutting Edge Jobs	15.95	____
____ 95 Mistakes Job Seekers Make and How to Avoid Them	13.95	____
____ 100 Great Jobs and How to Get Them	17.95	____
____ 101 Ways to Recession-Proof Your Career	14.95	____
____ 225 Best Jobs for Baby Boomers	16.95	____
____ 250 Best Jobs Through Apprenticeships	24.95	____
____ 300 Best Jobs Without a Four-Year Degree	16.95	____
____ About.com Guide to Job Searching	17.95	____
____ America's Top 100 Jobs for People Without a Four-Year Degree	19.95	____
____ America's Top Jobs for People Re-Entering the Workforce	19.95	____
____ Best Entry-Level Jobs (annual)	16.95	____
____ Best Jobs for the 21st Century	19.95	____
____ But What If I Don't Want to Go to College?	16.95	____
____ Career Change	14.95	____
____ Change Your Job, Change Your Life	21.95	____
____ Cool Careers for Dummies	19.99	____
____ Directory of Executive Recruiters	59.95	____
____ Five Secrets to Finding a Job	12.95	____
____ How to Get a Job and Keep It	16.95	____
____ How to Succeed Without a Career Path	13.95	____
____ Job Hunting Guide: From College to Career	14.95	____
____ Job Hunting Tips for People With Hot and Not-So-Hot Backgrounds	17.95	____
____ Knock 'Em Dead	14.95	____
____ Me, Myself, and I, Inc.	17.95	____
____ No One Is Unemployable	29.95	____
____ No One Will Hire Me!	15.95	____
____ Occupational Outlook Handbook 2008-2009	19.95/25.95	____
____ O*NET Dictionary of Occupational Titles	39.95/49.95	____
____ Quit Your Job and Grow Some Hair	15.95	____
____ Rites of Passage at $100,000 to $1 Million+	29.95	____
____ Top 300 Careers	18.95	____
____ What Color Is Your Parachute?	18.95	____
____ Your Dream Career for Dummies	16.99	____

Career Resources

Internet Job Search

____	100 Top Internet Job Sites	12.95	____
____	**America's Top Internet Job Sites**	19.95	____
____	Best Career and Education Websites	12.95	____
____	Career Exploration On the Internet	24.95	____
____	**Directory of Websites for International Jobs**	19.95	____
____	e-Resumes	16.95	____
____	Guide to Internet Job Searching	15.95	____
____	Haldane's Best Employment Websites for Professionals	15.95	____
____	Job Seeker's Online Goldmine	13.95	____

Resumes and Letters

____	101 Great Tips for a Dynamite Resume	13.95	____
____	**201 Dynamite Job Search Letters**	19.95	____
____	Adams Cover Letter Almanac	17.95	____
____	Adams Resume Almanac	17.95	____
____	Best KeyWords for Resumes, Cover Letters, & Interviews	17.95	____
____	**Best Resumes and CVs for International Jobs**	24.95	____
____	Best Resumes for $100,000+ Jobs	24.95	____
____	Best Resumes for People Without a Four-Year Degree	19.95	____
____	Best Cover Letters for $100,000+ Jobs	24.95	____
____	**Blue-Collar Resume and Job Hunting Guide**	15.95	____
____	Competency-Based Resumes	13.99	____
____	Cover Letter Magic	16.95	____
____	Cover Letters for Dummies	16.99	____
____	Cover Letters That Knock 'Em Dead	12.95	____
____	Create Your Digital Portfolio	19.95	____
____	Directory of Professional Resume Writers	17.95	____
____	Expert Resumes for Baby Boomers	16.95	____
____	Expert Resumes for Career Changers	16.95	____
____	Expert Resumes for Computer and Web Jobs	16.95	____
____	Expert Resumes for Managers and Executives	16.95	____
____	Expert Resumes for People Returning to Work	16.95	____
____	Gallery of Best Cover Letters	18.95	____
____	Gallery of Best Resumes	18.95	____
____	**Haldane's Best Cover Letters for Professionals**	15.95	____
____	**Haldane's Best Resumes for Professionals**	15.95	____
____	**High Impact Resumes and Letters**	19.95	____
____	Internet Resumes	14.95	____
____	**Military-to-Civilian Resumes and Letters**	21.95	____
____	**Nail the Cover Letter!**	17.95	____
____	**Nail the Resume!**	17.95	____
____	No-Nonsense Cover Letters	14.99	____
____	No-Nonsense Resumes	14.99	____
____	Resume Shortcuts	14.95	____
____	**Resume, Application, and Letter Tips for People With Hot and Not-So-Hot Backgrounds**	17.95	____
____	Resumes for Dummies	16.99	____
____	Resumes That Knock 'Em Dead	12.95	____

____ The Savvy Resume Writer   12.95 _____
____ Step-By-Step Resumes   19.95 _____
____ Winning Letters That Overcome Barriers to Employment   17.95 _____
____ World's Greatest Resumes   14.95 _____

Networking

____ **Dynamite Telesearch**   12.95 _____
____ Endless Referrals   16.95 _____
____ Fine Art of Small Talk   16.95 _____
____ Golden Rule of Schmoozing   12.95 _____
____ Great Connections   11.95 _____
____ How to Work a Room   14.00 _____
____ Little Black Book of Connections   19.95 _____
____ Masters of Networking   16.95 _____
____ Never Eat Alone   24.95 _____
____ One Phone Call Away   24.95 _____
____ Power Networking   14.95 _____
____ **The Savvy Networker**   13.95 _____
____ Shortcut Your Job Search   12.95 _____
____ Work the Pond!   15.95 _____

Dress, Image, and Etiquette

____ Business Etiquette for Dummies   21.99 _____
____ Dressing Smart for Men   16.95 _____
____ Dressing Smart for the New Millennium   15.95 _____
____ Dressing Smart for Women   16.95 _____
____ Power Etiquette   15.95 _____
____ You've Only Got Three Seconds   15.00 _____

Military in Transition

____ Expert Resumes for Military-to-Civilian Transition   16.95 _____
____ Jobs and the Military Spouse   17.95 _____
____ **Military-to-Civilian Resumes and Letters**   21.95 _____
____ Military-to-Civilian Career Transition Guide   15.95 _____
____ Military to Federal Career Guide   38.95 _____
____ Military Spouse's Complete Guide to Career Success   17.95 _____
____ **Military Transition to Civilian Success**   21.95 _____

Ex-Offenders and Re-Entry Success

____ 9 to 5 Beats Ten to Life   15.00 _____
____ 99 Days and a Get Up   9.95 _____
____ **Best Resumes and Letters for Ex-Offenders**   19.95 _____
____ Ex-Offender Recovery and Re-Entry Guides   33.95 _____
____ **Ex-Offender's Job Hunting Guide**   17.95 _____
____ Ex-Offender's Job Search Companion   11.95 _____
____ **Ex-Offender's Quick Job Hunting Guide**   9.95 _____
____ Houses of Healing   12.00 _____
____ How to Do Good After Prison   14.95 _____

Career Resources

	Item	Price	
____	Interview Skills Survival Guide for Ex-Offenders	12.95	____
____	Job Search Survival Guide for Ex-Offenders	12.95	____
____	Job Smarts and Survival Curriculum	85.95	____
____	Life Without a Crutch	7.95	____
____	Man, I Need a Job	7.95	____
____	Putting the Bars Behind You Survival Guides	59.95	____
____	Quick Job Search for Ex-Offenders	7.95	____

Changing Addictive and Not-So-Hot Behaviors

	Item	Price	
____	The Addictive Personality	14.95	____
____	Angry Men	14.95	____
____	Angry Women	14.95	____
____	Denial Is Not a River in Egypt	13.95	____
____	How to Quit Drugs for Good!	16.95	____
____	Managing Teen Anger and Violence	19.95	____
____	Passages Through Recovery	14.95	____
____	Sex, Drugs, Gambling and Chocolate	15.95	____
____	Stop the Chaos	12.95	____
____	The Truth About Addiction and Recovery	14.00	____
____	Understanding the Twelve Steps	12.00	____
____	You Can Heal Your Life	12.95	____

Government and Security Jobs

	Item	Price	
____	Book of U.S. Government Jobs	22.95	____
____	**Complete Guide to Public Employment**	19.95	____
____	Federal Applications That Get Results	23.95	____
____	FBI Career Guide	15.00	____
____	FBI Careers	19.95	____
____	Federal Law Enforcement Careers	19.95	____
____	Post Office Jobs	19.95	____
____	Ten Steps to a Federal Job	39.95	____

International and Travel Jobs

	Item	Price	
____	Back Door Guide to Short-Term Job Adventures	21.95	____
____	Big Guide to Living and Working Overseas	49.95	____
____	Careers in International Affairs	24.95	____
____	How to Get a Job in Europe	21.95	____
____	International Jobs	19.00	____
____	International Job Finder	19.95	____
____	**Jobs for Travel Lovers**	19.95	____
____	Teaching English Abroad	19.95	____
____	Work Worldwide	14.95	____
____	Work Your Way Around the World	19.95	____

ASSESSMENT INSTRUMENTS

	Item	Price	
____	Ability Explorer	42.95	____
____	Barriers to Employment Success Inventory	45.95	____

	Career Exploration Inventory	36.95	
____	Career Exploration Inventory	36.95	____
____	College Survival and Success Scale	41.95	____
____	Individual Employment Plan	37.95	____
____	Int4erview Style Inventory	35.95	____
____	Job Survival and Success Scale	40.95	____
____	O*NET Career Interests Inventory	35.95	____
____	O*NET Career Values Inventory	35.95	____
____	Transferable Skills Scale	37.95	____
____	Transition-to-Work Inventory	37.95	____

VIDEOS/DVDs

Interview, Networking, and Salary

____	Best 10¼ Tips for People With a Not-So-Hot Past	98.00	____
____	Build a Network for Work and Life	99.00	____
____	Common Mistakes People Make in Interviews	79.95	____
____	Exceptional Interviewing Tips	79.00	____
____	Extraordinary Answers to Interview Questions	79.95	____
____	Extreme Interview	69.00	____
____	Getting Good Answers to Tough Interview Questions	129.00	____
____	Interviewing for a Job	79.95	____
____	Interview to Win Your First Job	99.00	____
____	Interviewing: Your Key to Employment	129.00	____
____	Job Interview Tips and Techniques	109.00	____
____	Landing the Job: The Interview	108.00	____
____	Make a First Good Impression	129.00	____
____	Networking Your Way to a New Job	129.00	____
____	Seizing the Job Interview	79.00	____
____	Quick Interview and Salary Negotiations Video	149.00	____
____	Why Should I Hire You?	99.00	____

Dress and Image Videos

____	Head to Toe	98.00/108.00	____
____	Tips & Techniques to Improve Your Total Image	98.00/108.00	____

Resumes, Applications, and Cover Letter Videos

____	Building the Right Resume and Cover Letter	129.00	____
____	The Complete Job Application	99.00	____
____	How Do You Put It On Paper?	108.00	____
____	Landing the Job: Resumes and Cover Letters	108.00	____
____	Quick Resume and Cover Letter Video	149.00	____
____	Resumes, Cover Letters, and Portfolios	98.00	____

Attitude, Motivation, and Empowerment Videos

____	Down But Not Out	129.00	____
____	First Impressions	89.95	____

Career Resources

____	Get Motivated!	69.00 ____
____	Leadership for the New Millennium and Beyond	149.00 ____
____	Looking for Work With Attitude Plus	99.00 ____
____	Motivation and Goal Setting	99.00 ____
____	A New Attitude	99.00 ____

SUBTOTAL ____

Virginia residents add 5% sales tax ____

POSTAGE/HANDLING ($5 for first
product and 8% of SUBTOTAL) $5.00

8% of SUBTOTAL -------------------------------------- ____
(Include an additional 10% if shipping outside
the continental United States) -------------------------- ____

TOTAL ENCLOSED ---------------------- ____

SHIP TO:

NAME _____

ADDRESS _____

_____

_____

PAYMENT METHOD:

❏ I enclose check/money order for $ _____ made payable to IMPACT PUBLICATIONS.

❏ Please charge $ _____ to my credit card:
   ❏ Visa   ❏ MasterCard   ❏ American Express   ❏ Discover

Card # _____ Expiration date: ____/____

Signature _____

Thousands of resources available online: www.impactpublications.com

Your One-Stop Career, Life Skills, and Travel Centers

Books, DVDs, posters, games, pamphlets, and articles on anger management, addiction, recovery, mental health, jobs, careers, education, travel, military, ex-offenders, and much more!

www.impactpublications.com

www.exoffenderreentry.com

www.veteransworld.com

www.ishoparoundtheworld.com